wireWORK

AN ILLUSTRATED GUIDE TO THE ART OF WIRE WRAPPING

DALE "COUGAR" ARMSTRONG

INTERWEAVE
interweave.com

Interweave Press LLC
201 East Fourth Street
Loveland, Colorado 80537 USA
interweave.com

Printed in China by Asia Pacific Offset

Library of Congress Cataloging-in-Publication Data

Armstrong, Dale.
  Wirework : an illustrated guide to the art of wire wrapping / Dale
"Cougar" Armstrong ; editor, Jamie Hogsett.
      p. cm.
  Includes index.
  ISBN 978-1-59668-290-0 (pbk. with DVD)
  ISBN 978-1-59668-088-3 (pbk.)
  ISBN 978-1-59668-921-3 (eBook)
  1. Jewelry making. 2. Wire craft. I. Hogsett, Jamie, 1978- II.
Title.
  TT212.A77 2009
  739.27--dc22

                    2008054463

10 9 8 7 6 5 4 3 2

DESIGNER: KARLA BAKER
PHOTOGRAPHY: JOE COCA
STEP PHOTOGRAPHY: DALE ARMSTRONG
PHOTO STYLING: PAMELA CHAVEZ
PRODUCTION: KATHERINE JACKSON
VIDEO STUDIO MANAGER: GARRETT EVANS
VIDEO PRODUCER: RACHEL LINK

ACKNOWLEDGMENTS

I would like to thank several people for their help in making this book a reality:

Jane Mobley for providing the key that opened my mind to a past life. Dottie for her encouragement. My good friend and rock buddy Scott, thanks for being my personal "doorman" (helping to open so many), listening to me vent, and great music. Dearest "Scrimshaw Mary," thanks for always being there to listen and reflect things back to me so I can better understand my own words. To my supportive husband, Charlie (my personal lapidary), and my fabulous daughter, Skye, so much love and so many thanks for putting up with me during this wild ride (warning: it's not over!). Mom, thanks for showing me which rocks to pick-up when I was a kid. Thanks also to the wonderful staff at Interweave for their awesome patience and for working *with* me, especially my editors, Jamie Hogsett, Rebecca Campbell, and Tricia Waddell.

Most of all, I'd like to extend a huge thank-you to ALL of the students I have had the honor of working with throughout the years. When I teach, you may think you are getting the best of the situation—actually, I am! I listen to your design and technique desires, watch how different people work, formulate projects according to your requests, and as a result have become a better teacher. YOU are the reason for this book.

TABLE **OF CONTENTS**

ACKNOWLEDGMENTS 3

FOREWORD 7

INTRODUCTION 9

CHAPTER 1:
WIRED WORDS 10

Wire 12

Tools and Their Techniques 14

CHAPTER 2:
RINGS 18

Ring Basics 20

Free-form Orbit Ring 22

Crystal Wave Ring 26

Filigree Pearl Ring 32

CHAPTER 3:
BRACELETS 38

Bracelet Basics 40

Chevron Bracelet Base 44

Ornate Cabochon
Bracelet Topping 48

Beads All Around Clasp Bangle 54

CHAPTER 4:
EARRINGS 62

Earring Basics 63

Angel Chandelier Earrings 64

Gem Drop Earrings 68

Sparkle Earrings 76

CHAPTER 5:
PENDANTS AND NECKLACES 82

Pendant and Necklace Basics 83

Mixed-wire Cabochon Fish Pendant 84

Orbit Prong Gemstone Pendant 88

Drop Necklace Base Design 99

Gemstone/Cabochon Drop
for Attachment 104

Neck Collar 110

Bonus Project: Filigree Flower 114

INSPIRATION GALLERY 118

RESOURCES 126

INDEX 127

FORE**WORD**

It is the need to be creative, and to continually expand on that creativity, that makes us seek out those individuals who possess the skills and knowledge we admire and want to imitate.

It is the teacher who enables us to see that while imitating is a learning process, it is not as gratifying as tapping into our own inner creativity. It is the teacher who encourages us to expand on that acquired knowledge to find ourselves evolving beyond what we originally thought we were capable of doing.

Such a teacher is Dale "Cougar" Armstrong. Her philosophy is simple: Be creative! Take what you learn and turn it into your own style by thinking outside the box. Don't let the words "that can't be done" stop you from trying, from continually experimenting and most of all, from learning. One's individuality comes from not being afraid to continually strive for excellence and exploring all the possibilities of one's craft to its fullest.

Life molds all of us. Being able to take experiences, lessons, and knowledge, and blending them all together is the hard part. Dale has managed to do so by continually learning, experimenting, mentoring, and sharing her skills and techniques with many. And in doing so, she has acquired a following of students who respect her work, her advice, and her support in their own endeavors. She is a living example of a work still in progress because she strives to excel at what she does and take it a step further. This in turn keeps all her students striving to capture that essence as well. No matter how hard we work, it seems we are always a good ten steps or more behind Dale and her next idea.

This book is not a beginner's book, nor an advanced one. It is an accumulation of techniques and patterns for those individuals who need a bridge to the next step in the evolution of wire artistry. It has been written for those looking for more techniques, the answers to questions they have pondered at their own work benches, as well as a good dose of "what if" and "why not" in designing.

If you are expecting a "hold your hand" attitude, then you will be greatly disappointed. This book assumes you are beyond that, know your materials, know your tools, and are ready to go. So, enjoy this to the fullest. It's a great way to spread your wings and soar a bit higher in your creative life.

MARY W. BAILEY

INTRODUCTION

I have to tell you what a great time I had working on the designs in this book! It was fun to be able to write the details for some of my more elaborate pieces, knowing that somewhere, someone was—hopefully—going to be able to recreate the piece from the directions and then go off into their own world and make something fabulous as a result of now knowing how to bring their imagination to reality. This was one of my main reasons for writing this book.

I don't expect everyone to be interested in every design presented, but I do hope that some of the techniques shown will enable you to solve a mystery or two. I consider myself a technique instructor; to show how to utilize the skills taught, a finished product is necessary. Many of these designs have adjustable formulations so you can experiment with great results!

As a designer, I strive to formulate patterns that have a lot of versatility. As an instructor, one of my favorite rewards is watching my students take these opportunities and run with them, creating and combining variations that become their own designs. Throughout the book, you'll see images of jewelry created by my students after they learned the techniques and projects in this book. Some of the featured students have been working with "Cougarisms" for as many as nine years and some for just a few months. You can now see how my students inspire me!

A designer piece is just a beautiful combination of well-executed techniques and components. So grab your tools and wire, dig out some of the stones you've been saving until you knew what to do with them, and have a wonderfully creative day!

DALE "COUGAR" ARMSTRONG

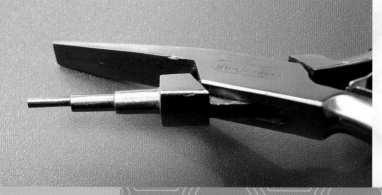

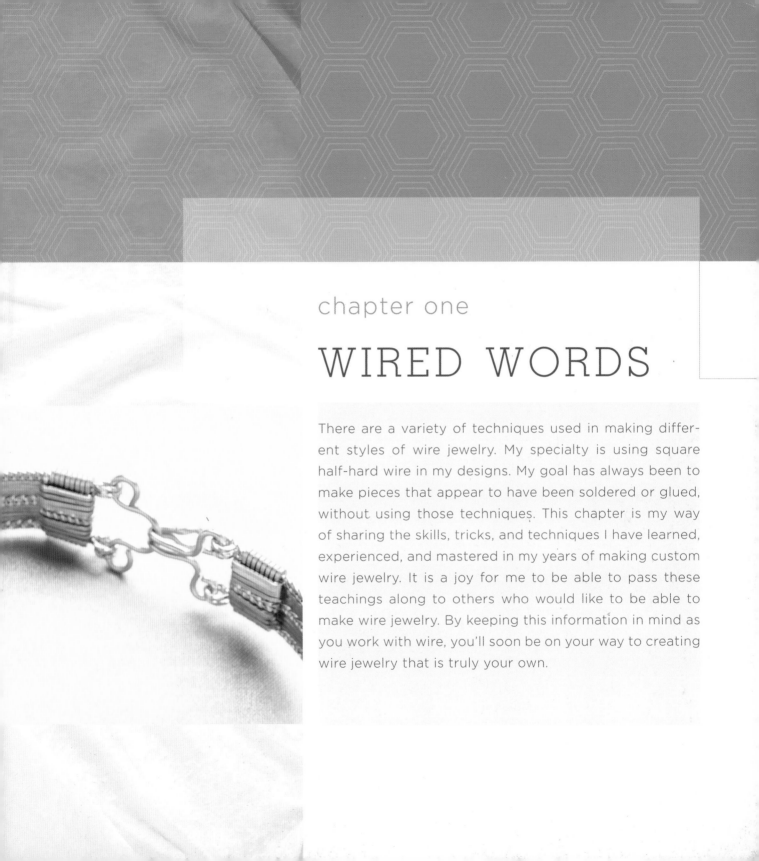

chapter one

WIRED WORDS

There are a variety of techniques used in making different styles of wire jewelry. My specialty is using square half-hard wire in my designs. My goal has always been to make pieces that appear to have been soldered or glued, without using those techniques. This chapter is my way of sharing the skills, tricks, and techniques I have learned, experienced, and mastered in my years of making custom wire jewelry. It is a joy for me to be able to pass these teachings along to others who would like to be able to make wire jewelry. By keeping this information in mind as you work with wire, you'll soon be on your way to creating wire jewelry that is truly your own.

WIRE

Whereas many designs and patterns utilize only round wire, the designs in this book are what have been termed "traditional wire jewelry," using no solder or glue. Instead, by using a variety of wire shapes and tempers, including square, half-round, half-hard, spring-hard, and occasionally round, creating anything is possible!

Over the years, I have done a lot of work in 14k and 18k solid gold. Obviously, this can be quite costly, so I have spent a lot of time formulating my wire patterns and designs to avoid as much waste as possible, thus the reasoning behind many of the "wired" choices I share with you.

If you think about it, we really don't bend wire, but rather we stretch the molecules, thus making it thinner, heating it as it stretches, and therefore hardening it. In some instances, we break the molecular cohesion of the wire causing it to snap or break.

HALF-HARD WIRE

Half-hard wire is powerful! Give it the proper direction, using the right tool, and it will do exactly what you tell it to do. Working with half-hard wire takes a bit more precision and confidence when making angles and shapes. It is important to use one motion, as opposed to hesitating and making several moves. (Multiple moves also give the potential for more tool marks on a finished item). My students and I have found that half-hard wire is more forgiving than soft. You can usually remove a badly made angle from a piece of half-hard, whereas with soft wire, a kink normally remains. Half-hard wire gives a nice, crisp look to angles as well as firm, smooth curves and will hold its shape for eons.

Working in dead-soft wire might be a lot easier than working with half-hard, and folks tell me that you need to put finished soft wire pieces into a tumbler to harden them. I have been a lapidary for years and tumble rocks. There is no way that I am going to

gauge	round	half-round	square
2g	●	◖	■
3g	●	◖	■
4g	●	◖	■
6g	●	◖	■
7g	●	◖	■
8g	●	◖	■
9g	●	◖	■
10g	●	◖	■
11g	●	◖	■
12g	●	◖	■
13g	●	◖	■
14g	●	◖	■
16g	●	◖	■
18g	•	◖	▪
19g	•	◖	▪
20g	•	•	▪
21g	•	•	▪
22g	•	•	▪
24g	•	•	▪
26g	•	•	▪

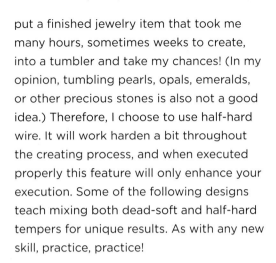

put a finished jewelry item that took me many hours, sometimes weeks to create, into a tumbler and take my chances! (In my opinion, tumbling pearls, opals, emeralds, or other precious stones is also not a good idea.) Therefore, I choose to use half-hard wire. It will work harden a bit throughout the creating process, and when executed properly this feature will only enhance your execution. Some of the following designs teach mixing both dead-soft and half-hard tempers for unique results. As with any new skill, practice, practice!

DEAD-SOFT WIRE

Dead-soft wire is very easy to manipulate and is fun to use when hand sculpting special swirls and curls. The temper makes it desirable to use when you want to "stretch" a wire until it hardens into a desired shape. I also like to combine soft with half-hard wire into different designs that need the power and stability of the half-hard along with the fluidity of the soft.

SQUARE WIRE

Working with square half-hard wire can offer a few challenges, keeping the wire "on the square" while making wraps, being the most common. Just remember that when wrapping a bundle, there are four sides— not just a back and a front—and that you have to make a 90° angle each time. There really are no good shortcuts. If you are going to put your valuable time and materials into a piece of work, take the necessary time to do it right! Binding pieces of jewelry that are in high-traffic areas, such

as bracelets and most rings, with square half-hard wire makes them much more durable. They will hold their shape better over the years and are a representation of the heirloom quality of your work. Square half-hard wire is also a great choice when connecting a pendant frame before creating a bail. The strength of this wire allows you to make fewer wraps to hold a piece together, allowing the bail to be closer to the top of a pendant for a cleaner finish. The most common square wire used in this book is 22-gauge square half-hard. It is an extremely versatile size and combines well with both 24- and 21-gauge.

HALF-ROUND WIRE

With half-round wire the front, or right side, is domed and the wrong, or backside, is flat. Half-round wire is basically used to bind wire bundles together. Regularly used on the frames of cabochon or cut stone pendants, earrings, and occasionally on rings, half-round takes up less space than square, so the frame will fit closer to the stone being set. The half-round wire most commonly used in this book is 20-gauge half-hard. Using this wire in a half-hard temper will make tight, neat bindings, and it will not have the tendency to wrap unevenly the way soft might. Believe it or not, using soft half-round wire can take more physical energy as you try to crimp it tightly enough to not appear sloppy! A larger gauge, such as a 16 or 18 (also half-hard), can work nicely on some bracelet and neckpiece designs, with the strength coming from the size and temper combination, instead of the shape.

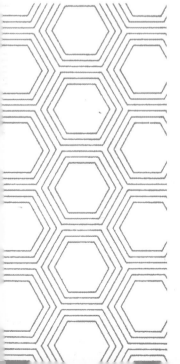

TOOLS AND THEIR TECHNIQUES:
THE RIGHT TOOL FOR THE RIGHT JOB

Kerf: 1. A groove or notch made by a cutting tool, such as a saw or an ax. 2. The width of a groove made by a cutting tool. 3. The material lost during a laser cutting or machining operation.

I like to use the term kerf to describe the amount of wire used by the surface of a tool as a shape or bend is executed, or the amount of wire taken up by a tool as a bend is made. An example of how this works is if you place flat-nose pliers directly on a mark to make a bend, the bend will finalize below the mark, due to the wire taken up by the pliers' kerf.

Although as a skilled wire jewelry artist, you already have your chosen tools, I'd like to share a few of my favorites with you and why I choose to use them.

PLIERS:
THE BASIC FOUR

It is fortunate to have such a wonderful variety of handheld, jewelry-making tools available, including many different types and sizes of pliers. Although a nice selection of specialty tools can be instrumental when executing many wire jewelry techniques, there are only four that I consider absolutely necessary for the style shown in the following designs. These four include: flat-nose, medium chain-nose, medium round-nose pliers, and a pair of medium angle flush cutters.

CHAIN-NOSE (SMOOTH JAW)

If I had to make a choice and only have one pair of pliers to use (along with cutters), I would choose a good pair of chain-nose pliers.

The jaws of chain-nose pliers come in quite a variety of lengths and widths. Their half-round exterior and smooth, flat interior make them perfect for starting small, tight loops. With chain-nose pliers, one can grasp a piece of wire at its very end and roll the wire around the outer, rounded jaw (round-nose pliers will more than likely slip off). Additionally, chain-nose pliers are used in many of the designs presented in this book when a "soft" angle is desired, meaning that an easy curve is desired instead of a hard angle. The flat interior of the chain-nose pliers makes them the perfect choice to control square wire bindings in small locations. Quite often, when giving the wire a desired direction over another single or group of wires, chain-nose pliers are used.

A good pair with a medium-size jaw is recommended, however a pair with fine needle jaws can be very handy to perform fine, detailed work. With experience, almost any technique can be executed with a nice pair of medium chain-nose pliers.

While looking at the different widths of both the inside and outside of the jaws of the chain-nose pliers, as they graduate from smaller to larger, one can determine which of the two sizes of pliers to use for a desired technique.

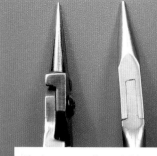
Chain-nose pliers (side vie

Chain-nose pliers

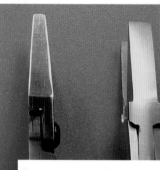
Flat-nose pliers (side view

Flat-nose pliers

FLAT-NOSE (SMOOTH JAW)

To create tight parallel wraps, a comfortable quality pair of flat-nose pliers is a must!

Flat-nose pliers are made in a huge variety of sizes. Their most important features are a large smooth interior and a sharply angled square tip. I use three different pair on a regular basis and make my choice depending on the technique I am executing. Smaller, sharp-ended flat-nose are wonderful for handcrafting prongs or when making serious 90° angles on smaller gauge or soft wire. Midsize flat-nose pliers are my choice when doing the majority of my work because they are so versatile. When working with very large wire—14-gauge and above—a heavier pair with thicker jaws fits my needs.

When choosing a pair of flat-nose pliers for yourself take into consideration that you will be using them about 75% of the time, so choose a pair with handles that fit your hand. For larger palms, I recommend longer handles because they take less power to open and close and therefore are kind to larger hands.

When looking at the sides of the jaws, consider the kerf (see page 14) when planning a bend. For example, when making a hook to start a binding over a single-wire-width bundle, make the hook near the very tip of the flats, as this location is similar in size to the wire width one is planning on wrapping over. When making a hook to go over a double-wire width, such as on a cabochon pendant, make the hook a little farther up the flat jaws due to the similarity in size to the double-wire width the hook will be going over.

ROUND-NOSE

Round-nose pliers are used mainly to hold or form a circular shape.

From the wide selection of round-nose pliers available, I have found that a pair with medium-size jaws is the one used most often in traditional wire-wrap designs. The tapering of the round-nose jaw can be very fine or blunt. The choice of which to use depends on the gauge of the wire and technique desired. Very-fine-tipped round-nose pliers are wonderful for head pin or light wire forming, but they cannot handle heavier gauged wire. Quite often a design will call for a wire to simply be held with the round-nose pliers, while the bending is actually done with the fingers.

FLUSH CUTTERS

A good pair of medium-weight angle flush cutters will suffice for about any wire gauge and with the tips shown later, make filing almost obsolete. Personally, I use four different-size cutters. Heavy for large gauge and pattern wires, medium for almost everything, midsize with longer thin tips for medium-gauge wire in small places, and little nippers for very small wire, head pins, and finishing work in tight places. Never use your good wire cutters on base metals!

Round-nose pliers (side view)

Round-nose pliers

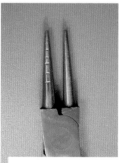

Scored round-nose pliers

> ### TIP
>
> To be able to repeat same-size bends, use a diamond file to score your favorite round-nose pliers jaws in the locations you use most often.

Angle flush cutters

SPECIALTY FORMING TOOLS

The variety of specialty tools for the jeweler is amazing! Quite often I will purchase a tool because I like the way it looks and figure out how I'm going to use it later. In this way I have found great uses and technique shortcuts for tools that were originally designed for other purposes. Although we could each have a huge tool collection, I like to keep things simple, and I actually use very few tools to accomplish many things. Here are some of my favorites, which can assist with executing the designs in this book.

SLIDING PIN VISE

Due to the thumb operation of this little gem, twisting short- to medium-length wires is quick and easy. I use this pin vise on wire gauges from 26 to 16. When twisting heavy long, or large amounts of wire, I recommend using a power drill/screwdriver with a keyless chuck. Twisting multiple wires at one time is much easier with a power tool and so much more fun!

3-STEPPED PLIERS

These are available with either a concave or a chain-nose jaw. I prefer the chain-nose jaw because when working with wire larger than a 20-gauge, the concave jaw can permanently nick the wire. These pliers are wonderful when making ear wires or a variety of bails and when working with several wires as one, such as link connections.

DOUBLE-BARREL PLIERS

I find these almost indispensable when making good pendant bails. They also make a great shaping tool when you need to form the base curve for tiny cabochons or faceted stones.

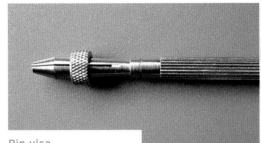

Pin vise

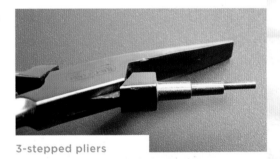

3-stepped pliers

Double-barrel pliers

3-stepped square tip pliers

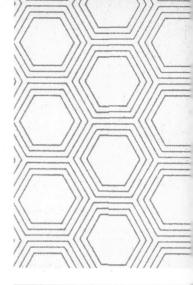

3-STEPPED SQUARE TIPS

These interesting pliers are used when forming wire latticework for frames. They are also wonderful shape formers for stones and cabochons with square edges.

ULTRA-FINE-POINT MARKER

Using a marker with as fine a point as possible when measuring and marking will help the symmetry of your work. The thicker a line, the more chance there is of being thrown off by a millimeter, which can be a lot! The end of the pen can also be used as a shaping item when forming a small U in situations that call for small round stones.

RING MANDREL

Because I personally prefer to use half-hard wire for most of my ring designs, I like a graduated smooth steel mandrel. Occasionally a ring design calls for the use of dead-soft wire because the wire hardens as it is forced down on the mandrel, therefore a smooth graduated surface is desired. A ring mandrel can also be used as a multi-size shaping tool when forming a wire frame around a cabochon or stone.

ARKEN-STONE

This wonderful little stone saves a lot of filing time. A natural sharpening stone such as this, in fine-grade grit, will file the edge of your wire while polishing it. What could be easier? Yes, I've used cup burrs and a variety of diamond files in an assortment of grades and sizes, but I prefer to keep things simple.

TAPE

There are many methods used to temporarily bind a wire bundle, or base. My favorite way is to use tape. A $1/4''$ (.6 cm) wide white quilter's tape is perfect for binding small projects or to use in locations that require a narrow piece of tape. (The green variety has too much adhesive.) For larger bundles/projects, you may choose to use a painter's tape, which is available in different widths. If the adhesive doesn't come off easily when the project is finished, just use a bit of denatured alcohol on a small rag. (This also works to remove unwanted ink marks.)

JEWELRY CLEANING MACHINE

Although you are probably using a polishing cloth to clean the wire as you straighten it, when a piece of jewelry is finished, it really needs to be fully cleaned. There are many pros and cons regarding mechanized jewelry cleaners. I prefer to use an ionic cleaner such as the Speed Brite. The chemical used is mixed with water and is safe on your hands. The machine has an automatic shut-off, and it is safe for use on opals, emeralds, and pearls (besides being affordable).

Now that I've shared my basic tips and techniques with you, we can move on to the fun part—the projects!

Marker

Ring mandrel

Arken-stone

chapter two

RINGS

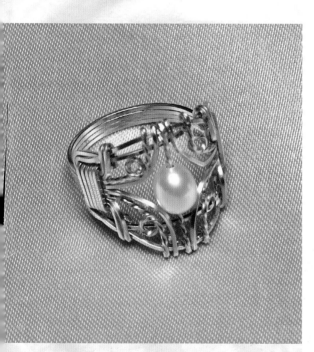

Rings are about the most popular piece of jewelry worn today. Most people purchase a ring for themselves because it is in a location on their body that they can see as they go about their activities. A beautiful ring brings attention from others to the wearer's hand. Several of my custom orders have been for people who use their hands exclusively and wished for a ring to purposely catch the eyes of an audience.

RING BASICS

Following are techniques that can be used with almost any wire ring project.

Beware of Sharp Points

When working on a ring design, continually try it on, checking for any sharp spots on the inside of the ring. If you find one, simply use a knife to carefully lift it from the ring. Either file it smooth or use chain-nose pliers to pull the burr off and form the wire end into a slight curve that heads back inside the ring. To finish, crimp the wire back into its original location.

Wrapping the Shank

I believe any ring with a shank of four or more wires needs to have the shank wrapped with half-round wire to keep the shank wires from eventually splitting apart with constant wear. A wrapped shank also gives a finished look to the ring and makes it silky smooth to put on and take off. Keep in mind that this shank wrap will take up a full size so size your rings accordingly and make the ring one full size larger than the desired finished size. Always use 20-gauge half-round half-hard wire to wrap a ring shank.

1

Use flat-nose pliers to form a hook on one end of the half-round wire. Place the hook on the ring shank as close to the side ring wraps as possible. Use your fingers to thread the half-round through the ring and pull very tightly around the shank, being careful to keep the shank wires in position without pulling them down next to each other **(Figure 1)**.

2

Use your fingers to continue to tightly wrap the shank **(Figure 2)**.

3

After the entire shank has been wrapped, use chain-nose pliers to secure the end of the wrap wire closely to the side ring wrap **(Figure 3)**.

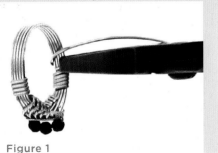

Figure 1

Figure 2

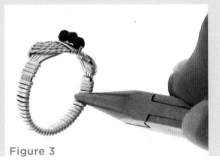

Figure 3

Proper Ring Sizing

Sizing a ring is often the most difficult part of the process.

To size, just drop the finished ring onto the mandrel. Do not force or push it down. Check to see what size the ring is and using a mallet, lightly tap the shank wrap all the way around the ring until it drops to the desired finished size. In this way, a wire ring can be sized to the quarter size. (It's almost magical!)

If a customer desires a one-of-a-kind ring already made and it's too small, simply remove the 20-gauge half-round shank wrap and replace it with 21-gauge half-round. If the ring is too large, replace the 20-gauge shank wrap with one made from 18-gauge half-round. Now isn't that easy? There are times when, as part of the design, I want to show part of the construction of the ring, so I only wrap half of the shank, in the middle.

RING SIZING CHART

IF THE SIZE YOU ARE MAKING IS:	MARK TO EACH SIDE OF THE CENTER:	CHECK THE TOTAL DISTANCE:
4 – 6	$^9/_{16}$" (1.5 cm)	$1^1/_8$" (3 cm)
6 – 8	$^5/_8$" (1.6 cm)	$1^1/_4$" (3.3 cm)
8 – 10	$^{11}/_{16}$" (1.8 cm)	$1^3/_8$" (3.6 cm)
10 – 12	$^3/_4$" (2 cm)	$1^1/_2$" (3.9 cm)

To use the above chart to make and size wire rings, add one full size to the desired finished size. This is the size you are making. After marking the center on a ring bundle, use the above chart to find and mark the distance on each side of the center mark—which is where to begin the side wraps on the ring. To double-check yourself, measure the distance between the two marks you made on each side of the center; it should equal the total distance listed on the chart.

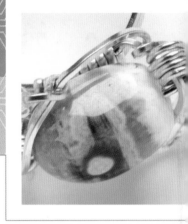

free-form orbit RING

This ring is an experiment using dead-soft wire. With this particular design, dead-soft wire works well due to its stretching/hardening properties. This is a seemingly simple design, with many possibilities!

materials

14" to 16" (35.5 to 40.7 cm) of 22-gauge square dead-soft wire

4" (10.1 cm) of 21-gauge round half-hard wire

9" (22.7 cm) of 20-gauge half-round half-hard wire

1 ocean jasper 8x12mm nugget (experiment by using any small-medium round, oval, nugget, or chevron bead)

2 faceted 4mm crystal rounds

tools

Wire cutters

Tape

Ring mandrel, smooth graduated steel preferred

Rawhide or nylon mallet

Flat-nose pliers

Round-nose pliers

Chain-nose pliers

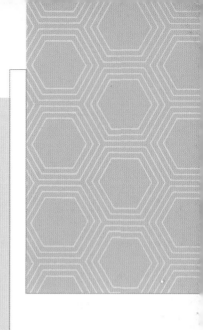

Finished Size (of the decorative top of the ring): ¾" × ⅝" (2 × 1.5 cm)

1

Straighten and clean all needed wires. Cut the 20-gauge half-round wire into three 3" (7.5 cm) pieces. Place the center of the 22-gauge wire at size 3 on the ring mandrel. Wrap this wire completely around mandrel three times (ending with three wires showing on the back and four on the front including two ends) and pull tightly. Force the ring down on the mandrel until it reaches two full sizes larger than the desired finished size, then pull the ends tightly. Note that the size you are making is one full size larger than the desired finished size (Figure 1).

2

Carefully remove the ring from the mandrel. Use one 3" (7.5 cm) 20-gauge wire to wrap the center of the ring by folding the midpoint of the wire around the center of the ring and wrapping from center toward each side. End with the wrap ends on the front of ring shape (Figure 2).

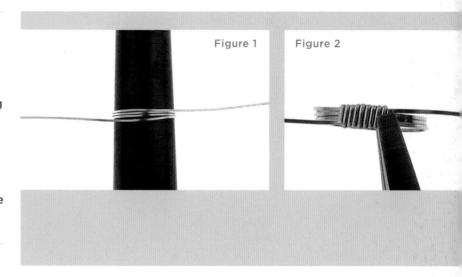

Figure 1

Figure 2

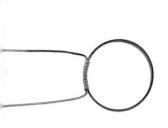

Figure 3

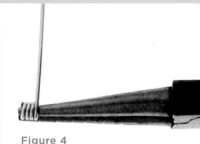

Figure 4

Figure 5

Figure 6

Figure 7

Figure 8

3

Replace the ring onto the mandrel and push it down to the making size. Hold the ring on the mandrel and bend the long wire ends from each side of wraps straight out toward the front at a 90° angle. Carefully remove the ring from the mandrel. Set it aside **(Figure 3)**.

4

Use round-nose pliers to make a spring shape four coils deep on one end of the 21-gauge round wire **(Figure 4)**. String the nugget. Make a mirror-image coil on opposite side of the bead heading down in the same direction as the first coil but rolled in the opposite direction, and trim **(Figure 5)**. To get the second side coil placed immediately next to the bead, start the coil away from the bead and then roll it back **(Figure 6)**.

5

Thread the coiled bead component onto the longer two wires on the front of the ring with the coils headed down toward the ring base. Bend each wire over its corresponding coil heading in opposite directions, one up and one down **(Figure 7)**.

6

Carefully tease each bent wire into an arched "orbit-shape," with one wire heading over the top of the bead and the other wire heading around the bottom of the bead. End by looping each end under the coil on its opposite side, locking in the orbit **(Figure 8)**.

Figure 9

7

Now get creative! Add beads and more orbits, coils, or zigzag shapes to the wires. For this design, string one 4mm round crystal onto each wire and finish by attaching the wire ends to opposite orbit wires and trim **(Figure 9)**.

8

Replace the ring on the mandrel and check the current size. Use 3″ (7.5 cm) of 20-gauge half-round wire to wrap the center/back of the ring shank and gently hammer on the shank wrap until the ring reaches the desired finished size.

Design variation using a handful of smaller crystals with one main center bead. Finished size (of the decorative top of the ring): $^3/_4$″ × $^1/_2$″ (2 × 1.3 cm).

crystal wave RING

The use of dead-soft wire in the construction of this ring shows how much a wire will change temper, or work harden, as it is manipulated through the design. Taking full advantage of this feature with small-gauge wire in tight places makes this an enjoyable project with many possibilities.

materials

25" (63.5 cm) of 22-gauge square dead-soft wire

24½" (62.2 cm) of 20-gauge half-round half-hard wire

3 faceted 3mm crystal rounds

tools

Wire cutters

Tape

Ring mandrel, smooth graduated steel preferred

Flat-nose pliers

Fine chain-nose pliers

Pin vise

Rawhide or nylon mallet

Finished Size (of decorative top of ring): ¾" × ¼" (2 × .6 cm)

1

Straighten and clean all necessary wires. Cut the 22-gauge wire into five 5" (12.6 cm) pieces and the 20-gauge wire into two 3" (7.5 cm) pieces and one 3½" (8.8 cm) piece; reserve the rest. Bundle the five square wires together with one flush end and tape near each end. Measure and mark the center of the bundle at 2½" (6.2 cm). Using the chart on page 21, measure and mark to each side of the center mark (according to the size you are making, which will be one full size larger than the desired finished size). Use one 3" (7.5 cm) half-round wire to wrap from one of these side marks away from the center four times to show. Trim just below the edge of the ring bundle. Use the other 3" (7.5 cm) half-round wire to repeat this wrap from the other side mark, keeping away from the center **(Figure 1)**.

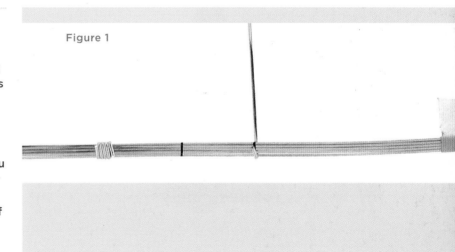

Figure 1

Figure 2

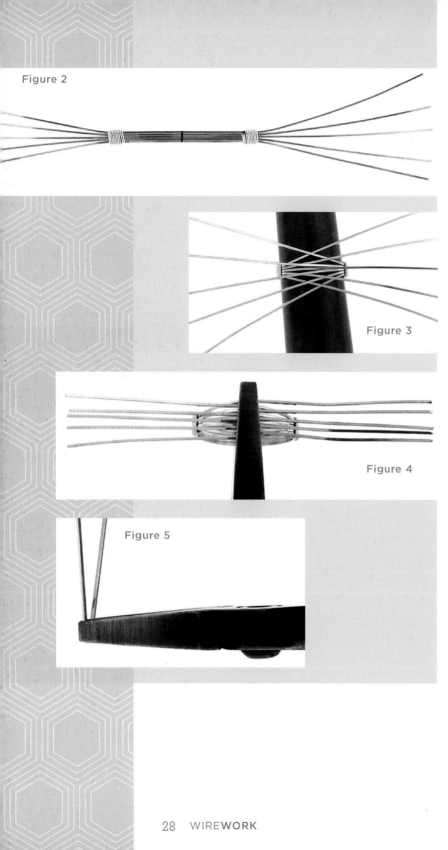

Figure 3

Figure 4

Figure 5

DESIGN NOTE

When making the wrap sets on either side of the center on a ring bundle, start them in opposite directions (one up and one down) to add strength to the ring base.

2

Remove the tape and slightly fan the five wires on each side as shown **(Figure 2)**.

3

Place back center mark against ring mandrel two sizes smaller than desired finished size and press on each side wrap with fingers to form a U shape. The wires will interlace on the front. Grasp the wire ends and pull tightly. Holding the ring firmly in position, force it down on the mandrel until it is two sizes larger than the desired finished size **(Figure 3)**.

4

Carefully remove the ring from the mandrel and use flat-nose pliers to flatten the interlaced wires at their center **(Figure 4)**.

5

Use flat-nose pliers to make an offset V at the center of the 3½″ (8.8 cm) of half-round wire (Figure 5).

6

Place the V just made onto the center of the interlaced wires and begin to wrap toward one side. Wrap twice to show (meaning you will see two complete wraps) and end mid-way up on the inside of the ring (Figure 6).

7

Place the tip of the jaw of chain-nose pliers on the outside of the half-round wire and bend the wire up toward the top of the ring, forming a platform to place beads on (Figure 7).

8

Use the half-round wire to string the three crystal rounds and continue wrapping toward the other side twice to show after the centered beads (Figure 8).

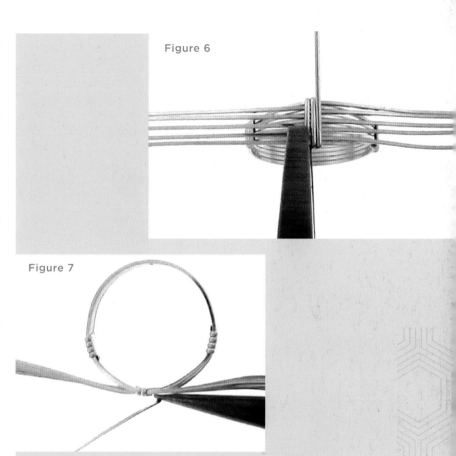

Figure 6

Figure 7

Figure 8

Figure 9

Figure 10

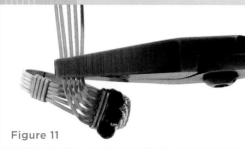

Figure 11

Figure 12

Use a pin vise to twist each individual wire on one side of the center **(Figure 9)**.

Looking at the ring on the side where it is obvious that the twisted wires will go down over a plain wire, use fingers to carefully move all wires down in a "wave" shape. Repeat with the untwisted wires on the opposite side, making wave in opposite direction **(Figure 10)**.

Use flat-nose pliers to grasp all wires on one side just above the ring's edge and bend as one over the edge so the wires lay on top of the edge. Repeat on the opposite side **(Figure 11)**.

Trim these wires until they are $\frac{1}{8}$" (.3 cm) longer than the edge they are going over. Working with all wires on one side as though they were one, use chain-nose pliers to put a slight arch into them, giving them the direction of heading down inside the ring **(Figure 12)**.

13

Use flat-nose pliers to tip these arched wire ends into the ring and when positioned, crimp firmly into place. If you have difficulty moving all the wires at once, do them each individually (Figure 13).

14

Place the ring onto ring mandrel and use the mallet to gently hammer on the waves (Figure 14). The pounding will reshape the ring as well as crush any sharp spots. Check the size and use 14″ (35.5 cm) of 20-gauge half-round half-hard wire to wrap the shank as described in Ring Basics, page 20.

Figure 13

Figure 14

Design variation using different colors of crystals and mixing metals (gold and silver). Finished size: ³/₄″ × ¹/₄″ (2 × 6 cm).

filigree pearl RING

Using the wonderful properties of half-hard wire—that it stays where you put it and will go in the direction you give it—makes this ring a lot of fun to get creative with. Hopefully after completing the pattern design, you will go off on your own adventures in ring making.

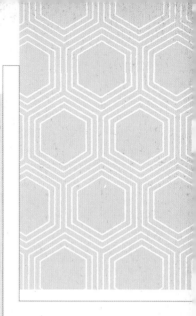

materials

47$\frac{1}{2}$" (120.7 cm) of 22-gauge square half-hard wire

10" to 16" (25.3 to 40.6 cm) of 20-gauge half-round half-hard wire

1 white 5x6mm pearl or other small specialty bead

Finished Size (of the decorative top of the ring): $\frac{3}{4}$" × 1" (2 × 2.5 cm)

tools

Wire cutters

Tape

Ruler

Ring mandrel, smooth graduated steel preferred

Thin dull blade

Rawhide or nylon mallet

Flat-nose pliers

Medium chain-nose pliers

Pin vise

Round-nose pliers

1

Straighten and clean all necessary wires. Cut the 22-gauge wire into eight 5" (12.6 cm) pieces, one 6" (15.1 cm) piece, and one 1$\frac{1}{2}$" (3.8 cm) piece. Bundle the eight 5" pieces together with one flush end and tape near each end. Mark across the center of the bundle at 2$\frac{1}{2}$" (6.3 cm). Use the chart on page 21 and determine the distance to mark on either side of the center for the side wraps. Use the 6" (15.1 cm) piece of square wire to make a set of five wraps to show on each side of the center, working from the marks out away from the center (Figure 1).

Figure 1

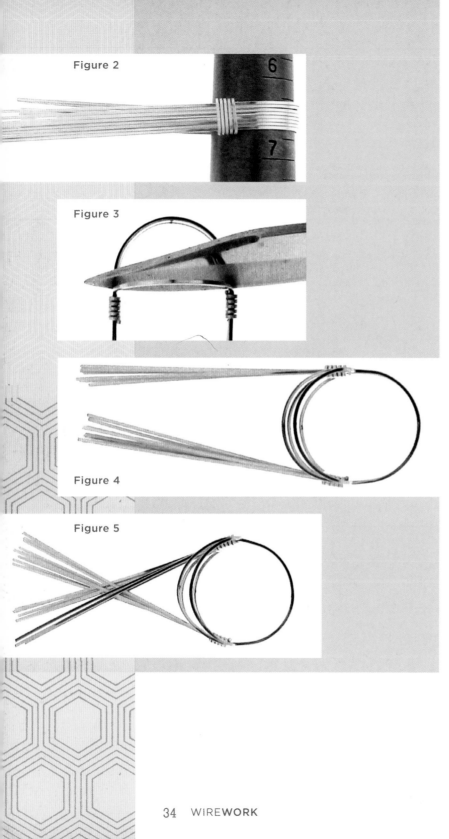

Figure 2

Figure 3

Figure 4

Figure 5

2

Remove the tape and place the back of the ring bundle at the point of the center mark on a ring mandrel three sizes smaller than the desired finished size. Press on the wraps, forming a U shape around the mandrel. Be sure the wraps are directly across from each other **(Figure 2)**.

3

Remove the ring from the mandrel and use a dull blade to slice between the first and second wires on one side of the ring shape. Use the blade to fold this wire up and over the wraps on the same side **(Figure 3)**.

4

Repeat Step 3 on the first wire on the opposite side of the ring shape. Return to the first side of the ring shape and repeat Step 3 with the second wire (one will be larger than the other) and repeat one more time on the other side, ending with two rings pulled on each side **(Figure 4)**.

5

Replace the ring on the mandrel and use a mallet to hammer the side wraps only, until they curve with the circle shape of the mandrel. This procedure will cause the front wires to interlace **(Figure 5)**.

6

At this point, do not worry about the size of the ring but check to see that it's not too much larger than where it began. (If the ring seems to be really large, move the shank wires back through the wraps a bit.) Remove the ring from the mandrel and use flat-nose pliers to hold the ring on one side wrap. Use fingers to move the interlaced wires back into their original positions. Repeat on the other side.

7

Holding the ring on one side wrap, use your fingers to bend the top two wires as though they were one wire, toward the side, making them parallel to the wraps (**Figure 6**). Repeat on all three other sides (**Figure 7**).

8.

Return the ring to the mandrel and firmly push the outer/larger circle toward the outside of the ring (**Figure 8**).

9

Working with one pair of wires at a time, place chain-nose pliers onto a pair of the paralleled corner wires just above the edge of the ring and bend them over the edge at a 90° soft angle (**Figure 9**).

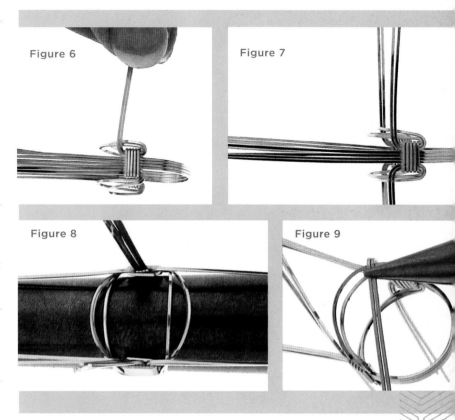

Figure 6

Figure 7

Figure 8

Figure 9

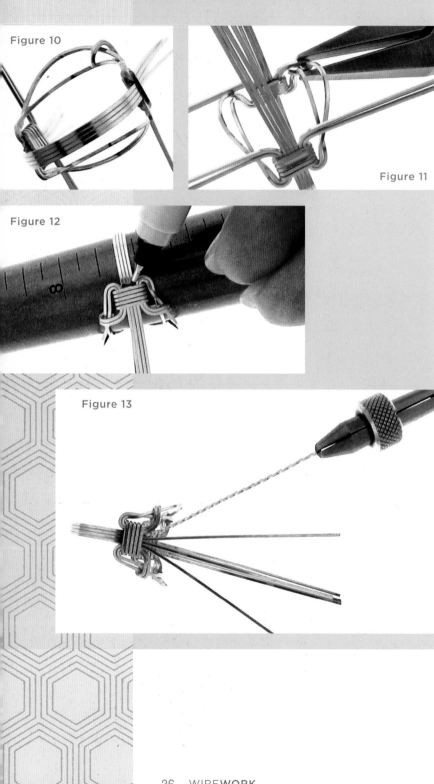

Figure 10

Figure 11

Figure 12

Figure 13

10

Trim these wires to $\frac{1}{8}$" (.3 cm) longer than the inside circle they are going over. Use chain-nose pliers to make a slight arch headed into the ring (**Figure 10**).

11

Use flat-nose pliers to tip the arched wire into the ring and over the two circular wires, locking them together. Repeat on all corners (**Figure 11**).

12

Drop the ring onto the mandrel and check the size where it falls. If the ring is too small, gently ease the ring down the mandrel until it is the size you are making. If the ring is too large, remove it from the mandrel and force the shank wires back through the wraps until it is smaller. Then replace the ring on the mandrel and slide it down until it is the size you are making. When the ring is the proper size, mark the shank immediately after the wraps on each side (**Figure 12**).

13

Slightly fan the four wires on either side away from each other. Use a pin vise to twist the outermost wire at each corner (**Figure 13**).

Implying Filigree

It's very important as the filigree steps are made and the wires connected that these wires are not pulled at all! Continually check the marks on the ring shank to be sure a wire has not been pulled before connecting it. If it has been pulled, put it back in place before locking the wire so the ring does not change size.

14

Place the tips of small round-nose pliers $\frac{1}{4}$" (.6 cm) away from the wrap and hold the wire while using fingers to bend it around the end of the pliers, forming a tiny loop (**Figure 14**).

15

Guide the wire following its natural curve to the outer ring and use chain-nose pliers to bend it over the ring at a sharp 90° angle. Trim this wire to ⅛″ (.3 cm). Use chain-nose pliers to make a half-loop at the end of the wire and then hook it over the outer ring, condense, and crimp it firmly. Repeat on all corners **(Figure 15)**.

16

Choose to twist or not to twist the precut 1½″ (3.7 cm) wire. Use chain-nose pliers to make a connection loop at one end and attach it to one of the ring's outer rings, centered between the just-created filigree loops. Add a pearl to this wire and attach the other end of the wire to the other outer ring **(Figure 16)**.

17

Decide whether or not to twist the last four wires and using the same techniques as above, decide where to place and connect them onto the outer circle, while locking the pearl/bead in the center **(Figure 17)**.

18

Wrap the shank as described on page 20 and then size.

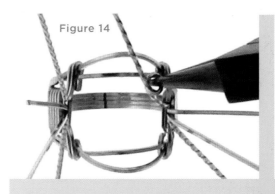

Figure 14

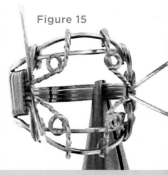

Figure 15

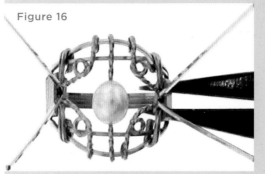

Figure 16

Figure 17

beaded rings

Jill Gentry used the techniques from the *Filigree Pearl Ring*, omitted the snap set stone and added a variety of beads and crystals to create these sparkling variations.

Filigree Pearl Ring, finished size 1″ × ½″ (2.5 x 1.3 cm)

chapter three

BRACELETS

Similar to rings, I have found that people purchase and enjoy wearing bracelets for themselves. The bracelets I teach are a more comfortable oval shape. Learning to formulate and create the Chevron Bracelet Base design (page 45) will enable you to turn just about anything desired into a wearable piece of "arm art." Taking beaded wire bracelets to the next level with Beads All Around (page 54) will give you the formulations needed to be able to incorporate a wider variety of components, shells, and gemstones into designs you may only have imagined possible.

BRACELET BASICS

Following are techniques that can be used with any wire bracelet project.

FORMULA: Most people like a bracelet that drops just to the top of the hand. When combined with the Hook-and-Eye Clasp (see page 42), the formula below will make a perfectly sized oval bracelet every time. For proper wrist measurement, use a cloth tape measure placed just over the small bone on the outside of the wrist. Bracelet Wire Length Formula = wrist + ½" (1.2 cm)

Shaping a Wire Bracelet

The following instructions teach you how to shape a wire bracelet so that it fits comfortably around the wrist.

1

Find an item that is just smaller than the curved shape desired and, by holding an end wrap on the object, bend the bracelet bundle two-thirds of the way around the shape. Move to the opposite end of the bundle and repeat, forming a rainbow arch into the bundle. Place the bracelet center on the shaping item and, by pressing on each side wrap, slightly arch the middle (Figure 1).

2

Continue to tease the bracelet bundle into shape by hand by reversing the same procedure used to straighten wire, pressing lightly up with the forefinger and down and over with the thumb. Work one side and then the other until the shape is close to being finished (Figure 2).

3

Return to the bracelet ends and working with each pair of wires as though they were one, slightly fan each outer two wires at the edges, away from the center wires. (These pairs of wires will now be referred to as "connection" wires.)

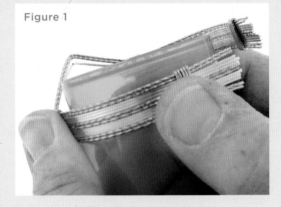

Figure 1

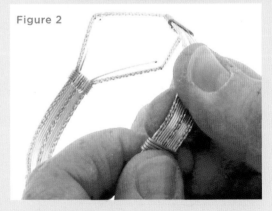

Figure 2

4

To finish the center wires at each end of the bracelet, use flat-nose pliers to firmly hold a set of center wraps in place and with finger, bend the cut center wires toward the back of the bundle at a 90° angle.

NOTE: Images in Steps 4 to 7 show how to finish the center wires in the center of a bracelet, but the technique is the same for finishing the center wires at the end of a bracelet (Figure 3).

5

Remove the flat-nose pliers and, for a soft angle, use fingers to continue bending cut center wires over the side wraps, leaving room under them for cutters. Trim the ends of these wires so they are about 1 mm longer than the wraps they are covering (Figure 4).

6

Use chain-nose pliers to put a slight downward arch into the ends of these trimmed wires (Figure 5).

7

Use flat-nose pliers to press the arch down over the side wraps, locking the ends in with no sharp edges (Figure 6).

8

Continue to work with each pair of connection wires, using fingers to bend them toward the front/outside of the bracelet. Trim each set so they are no shorter than they are but of equal length at each end (Figure 7). Using fingers instead of a tool at this point will reduce some of the stress on the connection wires.

9

Working with each set of connection wires, place round-nose pliers at the ends of each set and roll toward the back/inside of the bracelet, stopping when the open C shape made is centered above the end of the bracelet (Figure 8).

10

Use flat-nose pliers, placed on the entire unit to move the connection loops into proper position (Figure 9).

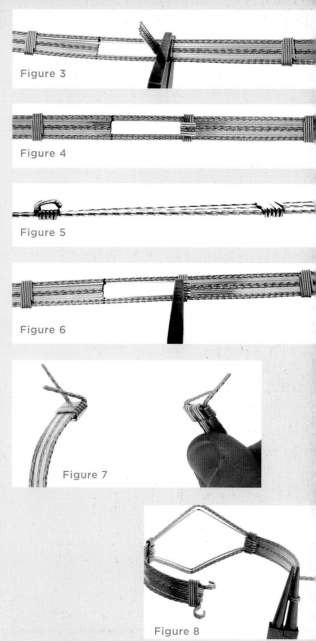

Figure 3

Figure 4

Figure 5

Figure 6

Figure 7

Figure 8

Figure 9

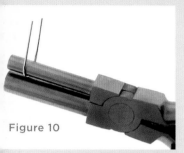

Figure 10

Figure 11

Figure 12

Figure 13

Figure 14

Figure 15

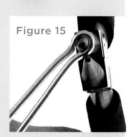

Figure 16

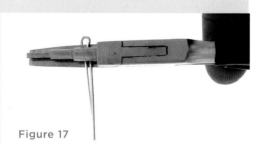

Figure 17

Hook-and-Eye Clasp:

The hook-and-eye clasp is perhaps the best type of clasp to use with the wire bracelet designs in this book. You'll need 16- or 18-gauge dead-soft round wire: 2″ (5.1 cm) for the eye and 2¾″ (7 cm) for the hook.

1

Center a 2″ (5.1 cm) piece of 18-gauge round dead-soft wire into the jaws of double-barrel pliers and shape an even U around the smaller barrel **(Figure 10)**.

2

Use round-nose pliers to form a loop on the outside edges of the U just made, completing the eye **(Figure 11)**.

3

Center a 3″ (7.7 cm) piece of 18-gauge round dead-soft wire near the tip of round-nose pliers. Form a very tight U over the tips of the pliers **(Figure 12)**.

4

By working the tip of the round-nose pliers around the U just made, "keyhole" the end of the hook, forming a lock **(Figures 13 to 16)**.

5

Place the hook into the largest on the 3-stepped pliers, with the lock end just outside the jaw **(Figure 17)**.

6

Roll the 3-stepped pliers until the lock end meets the straight end **(Figure 18)**.

7

Insert the end of the flat-nose pliers between the legs of the hook, just under the actual curve. Grasp the leg being held and bend out at a 90° angle. Remove the pliers, replace on the opposite leg, and repeat **(Figure 19)**.

8

Place the end of one leg into the tips of the round-nose pliers and roll the pliers to form a loop under and to the side of the hook. Repeat on the opposite leg **(Figures 20 and 21)**.

DESIGN NOTE

One of the beauties of using an independent hook-and-eye closure such as the one detailed in Bracelet Basics (page 40) is that a bracelet can be easily resized in a few moments by simply making a smaller or larger hook-and-eye clasp. In rare cases, when a customized bracelet is much larger than changing the size of the hook and eye will remedy, resizing is still an easy feat. When the correct size has been determined, just make a full set of wraps, as far behind one of the original clasp wraps as needed, and refinish the bracelet. If a bracelet is way too small, there is no choice but to take the order and custom create the desired bracelet.

Finishing a Bracelet

1

Insert the hook into the connection loops on one end of the bracelet, with the front/hook facing the front/outside of the bracelet. Use the tips of fine chain-nose pliers to grasp a connection loop two-thirds of the way around and roll the loop closed over the hook. Repeat procedure to connect the eye **(Figure 22)**. Placing the hook on the bracelet in this manner allows the wearer to easily put on and remove the bracelet by herself, plus the hook is now facing away from and not digging into the arm.

2

Clasp the bracelet closed and use flat-nose pliers and hands to finish shaping **(Figure 23)**.

Figure 18

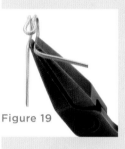
Figure 19

Figure 20

Figure 21

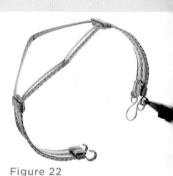
Figure 22

Figure 23

chevron bracelet BASE

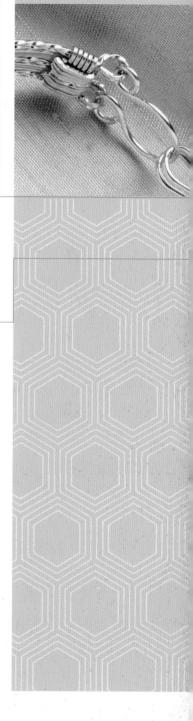

This basic all-wire bracelet, with an opening on which to attach a variety of "toppings" (page 48), has so many different possibilities and variations that it is a must-have in every wire jewelry designer's knowledge base. When this bangle is made without the chevron opening, it is a wonderful unisex bracelet.

materials

Note that this bracelet can be made with 22-, 21-, or 20-gauge square half-hard wire

12 pieces of Formula (F) length wires

19" (48.3 cm) of wire for wraps

4³/₄" (12 cm) of 18- or 16-gauge round dead-soft wire for clasp

tools

Flat-nose pliers

Medium chain-nose pliers

Round-nose pliers

Cutters

Tape

Ruler

Fine-point marker

Power wire twister

Split-ring opener

Finished Size: band is ³/₈" (1 cm) wide, clasp is 1 ¹/₈" × ¹/₂" (3 × 1.3 cm)

FORMULA: The following directions were written using a combination of six silver and six gold-filled 22-gauge bracelet length wires, therefore the wrap wires are 4¾" (12 cm) long. If the bracelet is made with a larger or smaller number of base wires, adjust the wrap wire lengths accordingly. Bracelet Wire Length Formula = wrist + ½" (1.2 cm)

DESIGN NOTE

As the creator, you'll decide which metals to use and what pattern you would like. My only recommendations are that when deciding how many wires to twist, you do not twist them all (as it is difficult to properly bundle and bind a large group of twisted wires) and that at least one twisted wire is added to the outer edges of this bracelet (as the twisted wire will keep your bindings from slipping when they are made tightly enough). Place one piece of twisted wire, twisted using a drill on forward mode, next to one twisted in reverse mode to form a herringbone look!

CHEVRON BRACELET BASE

1

Straighten, clean, then measure and cut all of the necessary wires. Individually twist two or more pieces of F-length wire. Plan the bracelet pattern, bundle all F wires with one flush end (remembering to place one twisted wire at each edge), and tape close to each end. Using ¼" (.6 cm) quilter's tape works well in this case, as it is thin **(Figure 1)**.

2

Place the bracelet bundle alongside a ruler with the flush end at the number zero. Measure from the flush end to ½" (1.2 cm) and mark across the entire bracelet bundle. Rotate the bundle so the back is still showing and place the shortest wire of the uneven end at the zero; measure ½" (1.2 cm) and mark. Measure the distance between the two marks just made to find the center and mark. Place the center mark on any whole number and measure and mark 1⅛" (2.8 cm) to either side of the center (for bracelet F wires that are 6½" (16.4 cm) or shorter, make this measurement an even 1" (2.5 cm) to either side of the center). This side, with the marks, is now the back side of the bundle.

3

Starting at the flush end of the bracelet bundle, use flat-nose pliers and a 4³/₄" (12 cm) wrap wire to make a hook that will cover the entire width of the bundle, minus two wires. Following the directions on the chart (page 57), wrap from the first mark at the flush end and work toward the center, five times to show, trim the wrap wire two wires short of the edge. Following the same hook and trim procedure at the second mark, work back toward the first wrap, five times to show. At the third mark, wrap five times to show toward the uneven end and finish wrapping from the final mark back toward the center,

Figure 1

five times to show (Figure 2). Due to the way this bracelet is finished, it is important for the wrap wires to go across the entire bundle minus two wires.

4

Remove all tape. Use fine chain-nose pliers to carefully lift and then cut the center wires three wires in from the edges near the center mark (Figure 3).

5

Use flat-nose pliers to firmly hold a set of center wraps in place and with fingers, bend the cut center wires toward the back of the bundle at a 90° angle (Figure 4).

6

Remove the flat-nose pliers and, for a soft angle, use fingers to continue bending the cut center wires over the side wraps, leaving room under them for cutters. Trim the ends of these wires so they are about 1 mm longer than the wraps they are covering (Figure 5).

7

Use chain-nose pliers to put a slight downward arch into the ends of these trimmed wires (Figure 6).

8

Use flat-nose pliers to press the arch down over the side wraps, locking the ends in with no sharp edges (Figure 7).

9

To make a more defined chevron opening, support the bracelet bundle by holding onto the side wraps; at the center mark on the center frame, use a pair of split-ring openers to pull the opening into a chevron shape. Or, for a softer look, simply use the thumb and forefinger on each hand and pull simultaneously. If the opening is too large, simply push it back down to the desired size (Figure 8).

10

To finish the Bracelet Base, see Bracelet Basics, page 40.

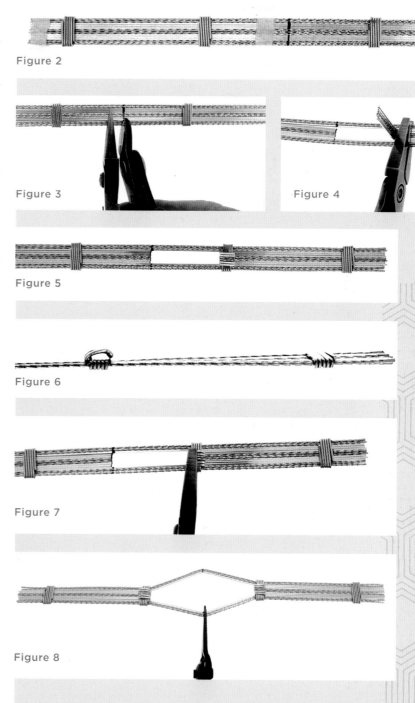

Figure 2

Figure 3

Figure 4

Figure 5

Figure 6

Figure 7

Figure 8

ornate cabochon bracelet
TOPPING

The instructions that follow show just one of the many ways a cabochon can be wrapped and incorporated into a beautiful bangle bracelet. As with most of the directions in this book, the formula can be adjusted to enable the use of almost any shape or size cab. Deciding whether or not to use accent beads; changing the colors of wires used; imaginative combinations of rosettes, swirls, and tendrils; and of course the shape and color of the chosen cabochon will make each bracelet a new one-of-a-kind design!

materials

22-gauge half-hard wire for the frame (21-gauge and 24-gauge can also be used, depending on the gauge used in the base bracelet and the size of the cabochon)

16" of 20-gauge half-round half-hard wire for the side wraps

1 eudyalite 26x32mm cabochon (or cabochon of your choice)

4 rhodolite garnet 5x7mm faceted ovals (or accent beads of your choice)—optional

Finished Size (of the topping): 1¾" × 1⅞" (4.5 × 4.9 cm)

tools

Flat-nose pliers

Medium chain-nose pliers

Round-nose pliers

Cutters

Tape

Ruler

Fine-point marker

Power wire twister

Pin vise

FORMULA: Wire Length = circumference of cab divided by two + 3" (7.5 cm). Amount of wires = enough wires needed to cover the entire side/girdle of the cab plus two more. Two sets of the Amount wires are needed, plus two 2" (5.1 cm) wrap wires in the same gauge.

Figure 1

Figure 2

Figure 3

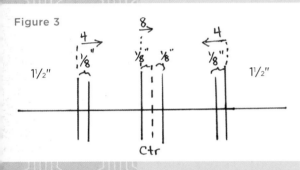

Figure 4

Figure 5

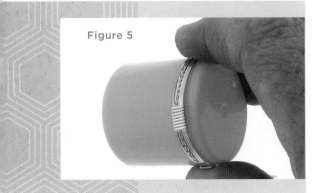

ORNATE CABOCHON BRACELET TOPPING

1

Plan the cabochon frame. Make measuring easy! Use a piece of tape with one turned-over edge and one straight cut edge. Place the straight cut edge on the girdle/side of the cabochon and roll the cabochon into the tape until the tape meets itself. Mark the tape where it meets the cut edge. Remove the tape, place it alongside a ruler, and measure it. Also find and mark the center of the cabochon length on the tape. This half measurement plus 3″ (7.5 cm) is how long the wires need to be. Start by straightening and cutting five wires to the necessary length. Holding the wires side by side, place the edge of the cabochon on top of them to see if more wires are needed to cover the girdle. When finished cutting the wires for one side, cut another set for the other side of the cab frame (**Figure 1**).

Example: If a cabochon is 5″ (12.6 cm) around, the necessary wire length is 2½″ (6.2 cm) + 3″ (7.5 cm) = 5½″ (13.8 cm). If the cabochon's girdle is 4mm thick, five wires should cover it, plus two, so the number of frame wires needed per side would be seven pieces, each 5½″ (13.8 cm) long.

2

Decide whether or not to twist a couple of the frame wires. (Twisted wires may be used to decorate the side of the frame.) Make two frame bundles, one for each side of the cabochon; place the necessary number of frame wires side by side with one flush end in the desired pattern and tape near each end. Place along a ruler and mark the center of each bundle (**Figure 2**).

3

Make a diagram of one half of the frame by using the example pictured, the length determined by the tape. (The size of the cabochon used doesn't matter; the measurements will be the same, unless using a much smaller cabochon, then cut the wrap sections by ¹/₁₆″ [.15 cm]). To make measuring easy, always place a mark on a whole ruler number, such as 3, and go from there (**Figure 3**).

4

Place the frame bundles alongside the diagram. Line up the center marks and transfer the remaining measurements from the diagram to the bundles. Use an 8″ (20.2 cm) piece of 20-gauge half-round to wrap the entire center section on each bundle eight times to show (begin and end the wraps midway up the bundle). Move to a mark at either end and, working toward the center, wrap each side section four times to show (**Figure 4**).

5

Create the frame. Remove the tape from the frame sides and choose a shaping item that is just smaller than the size of the cab. With the back of the frame (where the wraps begin and end) pressed against the shaping item, hold on to the wraps and bend each side of the frame to fit the side of the cabochon (**Figure 5**).

6

Place flat-nose pliers on one end of a frame so the edge of the jaw is just below an end wrap and bend the end of the frame toward the outside at about a 45° angle. Repeat on each end of each frame (**Figure 6**).

7

Fit the frame around the cabochon (remembering what position any twisted wires are supposed to be in) and on each side, tape ¹/₂″ (1.2 cm) up from where the frame joins (**Figure 7**). Do not make the frame too tight or there will not be enough play for the wire to pull in on the stone as the frame is completed.

8

Remove the stone. Use a 2″ (5 cm) square wrap wire to make a hook that will go over the entire joining of the frames and place it over the joint with the hook heading toward the back of the frame. Wrap from the joining up three times to show on the top and trim heading toward the back of the frame. Repeat on the opposite end, finishing the shape (**Figure 8**).

9

Remove all tape. On the back of the frame, place flat-nose pliers on the topmost wire immediately next to a center wrapped segment and bend in toward the open center at a 90° angle. Repeat at each side of a center wrapped area on the back side only (**Figures 9 and 10**). Always work from the center first, as the wire is pulling out from each end. If a bend is made at each top first, there will not be enough wire to pull at the center sections.

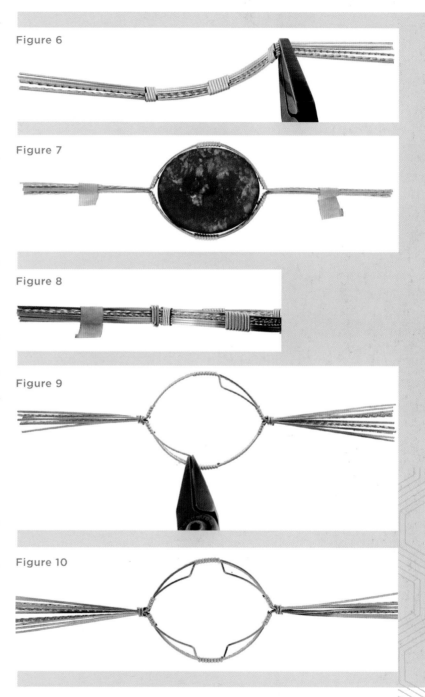

Figure 6

Figure 7

Figure 8

Figure 9

Figure 10

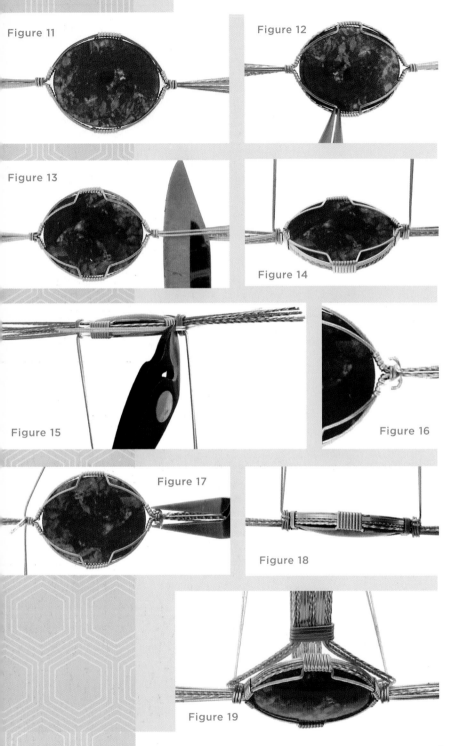

Figure 11

Figure 12

Figure 13

Figure 14

Figure 15

Figure 16

Figure 17

Figure 18

Figure 19

10

Turn the frame so the front is up and carefully fit the cabochon into the frame (**Figure 11**). On the front/top, use chain-nose pliers to repeat the procedure in Step 9, securely locking the cabochon into the frame (**Figure 12**).

11

Combine cabochon and bracelet. With the back of the framed cabochon facing up, at each end, use a dull blade to separate the last two wires from the rest of the bundle and bend them toward the back at a 90° angle (**Figures 13 and 14**).

12

On each side of each end, on the rear, separate the next two wires and bend them down toward the side of the framed cabochon (**Figure 15**). Trim each set so they are 1 mm longer than the end wraps they are heading over. Use chain-nose pliers to put a slight arch into each set of wires and then use flat-nose pliers to push each set over the wrap wires (**Figures 16 and 17**).

13

From the front of the bracelet, insert the framed cabochon, with the longer wires heading toward the back/inside of the bracelet. If the chevron opening is not large enough, pull it from the points to fit (**Figure 18**).

14

Bend each of the straight wires from the back up and over the main bracelet frame to settle the framed cabochon in place. Use chain-nose pliers to tease a curve from the tip of each wire, working it down so the wire curls toward the frame (**Figure 18**). Insert the curved wire into and around the frame a minimum of two times, using flat-nose pliers to secure it, and ending on the top/front of the bracelet frame. This prevents sharp wires against the arm and will be covered with decorations later (**Figures 19 and 20**).

15

Use a combination of beads, rosettes, swirls, and tendrils to decorate and further lock in the framed cabochon. To form a rosette, twist a square wire to give it a "diamond-cut look" and use fine chain-nose pliers to make a full, tight curl on the end of the wire. Use flat-nose pliers to roll the curled loop onto itself, keeping it flat. Continue rolling the wired loop around itself until it is as large as desired. In other words, a rosette is a spiral that has been tightly created using twisted square wire **(Figure 21)**.

Figure 20

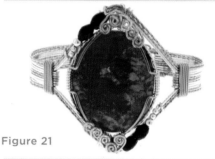

Figure 21

lapis slave bracelet

Modifying the *Ornate Cabochon Bracelet* design and adding a chained ring, K. Luttrell created a slave bracelet.

Bracelet circumference 7¼" (18.4 cm); bracelet topping 2³⁄₈" x 1" (6 x 2.5 cm); chain 4³⁄₈" (11.1 cm); decorative top of ring 1½" x ¾" (3.8 x 1.9 cm)

rhodochrosite swirls bracelet and earrings set

Sandra W. Wurm used a very large rhodocrosite cabochon to make her rendition of the *Ornate Cabochon Bracelet.*

Bracelet circumference 6⁵⁄₈" (16.8 cm); bracelet topping 1" x 2¼" (2.5 x 5.7 cm); earrings ½" x 1" (1.3 x 2.5 cm)

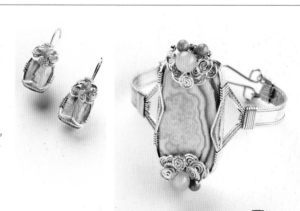

54

eads all around CLASP BANGLE

This design takes an all-wire bangle to new levels, showing how to dress it up by adding several rows of beads. Adding bead platforms above a strong base eliminates the challenge of how to keep the beads from "pulling down into" and misshaping a bracelet, or how to keep a consistent open space around them while forming and wrapping other bracelet designs. As always, the design possibilities are almost endless. For variations, make the design with a single bead wire through the center or use two bead wires spaced evenly within the width of the bangle. Of course, making this design as shown with a center focal bead is just an option.

Wire Length Formula (F) = wrist + $\frac{1}{2}''$ (1.2 cm)

materials

12 pieces of F-length 21-gauge square half-hard wire

30" (76.3 cm) of 21-gauge square half-hard wire for wrap wires

3 pieces of F length plus $\frac{3}{4}''$ (1.9 cm) 22-gauge square half-hard for bead wires

58 purple 4mm faceted CZ rounds

2 purple 8mm faceted CZ rounds

1 purple 9x14mm double-drilled CZ bead

tools

Flat-nose pliers

Medium chain-nose pliers

Fine chain-nose pliers

Round-nose pliers

Cutters

Tape

Ruler

Fine-point marker

Power wire twister

Split-ring opener

Finished Size (of the center section of the bracelet): $1\frac{5}{8}'' \times \frac{3}{4}''$ (4 × 1 cm)

BEADS ALL AROUND CLASP BANGLE

The following directions are a suggestion; the number of wires used depends on the desired bracelet width, and the bead shape and size can be adjusted according to the desired width and length.

1

Straighten, clean, measure, and cut all needed wires. Twist at least two but no more than six of the 21-gauge F wires. Place all the F wires side by side into the desired pattern, remembering to use a twisted wire on each outer edge. Place one 22-gauge bead wire in the fourth, the center, and the thirteenth positions in the bundle, making sure the wires are positioned so that the bundle has one flush end. Tape the bundle near either end **(Figure 1)**.

DESIGN NOTE

This design works well using either combination: 22-gauge square half-hard wire for the base and 24-gauge square half-hard as the bead wires, or 21-gauge square half-hard for the base and 22-gauge square half-hard as the bead wires (as used below). The 22-gauge/24-gauge combination works well with pearls, as they have smaller holes. Soft wire is not recommended, as it will not hold its shape as well as the bracelet base, and the bead platforms tend to move about, will be flimsy, and may break easily. Substituting round wire for the beads is not advised as round wire will not bind tightly into the bundle.

Figure 1

TIP

When planning the beads for this design, figure the bracelet length first and make an exact diagram as shown in Step 2. Place the desired beads on a piece of scrap wire and layout according to the space available on the diagram.

2

Place the flush end of the bundle alongside a ruler at the number zero. Measure in ½" (1.2 cm) and mark across entire bundle. (This is now the back of the bracelet bundle.) Rotate the bundle so the back is still showing and place the shortest wire on the uneven end at the number zero. Measure in ½" (1.2 cm) and mark. Now measure the distance between the two marks just made, find the center, and mark. Place this center mark on any whole number of the ruler, measure ⅞" (2.2 cm) to each side of the center, and mark.

NOTE: The ⅞" (2.2 cm) to either side of the center represents the distance across the arm. If making a bracelet with an F length of 6½" (16.4 cm) or smaller, use ¾" (1.9 cm) instead. Place one of these side marks on a whole number and measure ³⁄₁₆" (.5 cm) away from the center. Slide this new mark to a whole number and measure ⅞" (2.2 cm) toward the end and mark. Repeat on the other side of the center (Figure 2).

NOTE: If the F length is 8½" (21.5 cm) or longer, increase these ⅞" (2.2 cm) measurements to 1⅛" (2.8 cm).

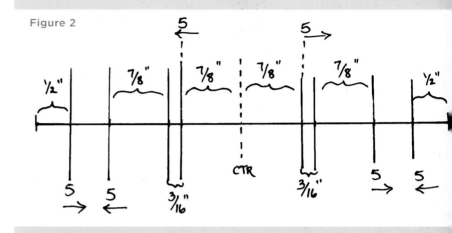

Figure 2

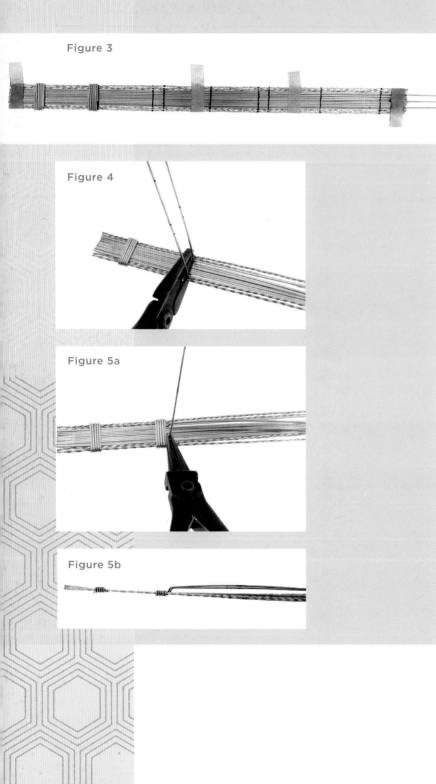

Figure 3

Figure 4

Figure 5a

Figure 5b

Use a 5″ (12.5 cm) wire and flat-nose pliers to make a hook long enough to go across the entire bundle width, minus two wires. (Due to the way this bracelet is finished, the first and last wraps need to begin and end almost across the entire bracelet width.) Begin wrapping at the first mark on the flush end of the bundle and wrap toward the center five times to show, remembering to end the wrap two wires shy of the edge. Following the diagram from Step 2, begin the next wrap at the second mark from the flush end and wrap away from the center five times to show (**Figure 3**).

Remove all tape and, with the bracelet bundle front/top facing up, use flat-nose pliers to hold the second wrap in place and slide index finger up and under the outer two longer bead wires from the bundle edge all the way back to the second wrap so the wires are sticking straight out from the bundle at a 90° angle on the front/top (**Figure 4**).

To create a bead platform, use fine-tip chain-nose pliers and grasp one of the bead wires at its base, immediately above the second wrap. While holding this wire with the tips of the pliers, use a finger to push the wire over the top of the jaw of the pliers at a soft 90° angle. Repeat this procedure on the second bead wire (**Figures 5a and 5b**).

NOTE: To determine how far up the jaw of the pliers the bead wire needs to be gripped depends on the size of the bead being used. Measure the distance from the hole to the table; this is how high the bead platform needs to be made.

6

Use one bead wire to string eight 4mm CZ faceted rounds. Use fine-tip chain-nose pliers, placed so the jaw edge closest to the beads is no farther than 1 mm away from the beads, to bend the bead wire back down into the bracelet bundle, at a 90° angle. (This negative space is necessary for the beads to be able to move a bit when the bracelet is shaped.) Repeat using the other bead wire (**Figure 6**).

7

To finish the bead platform, use flat-nose pliers to grasp the bead wire immediately under the bracelet bundle and bend toward the end of the bracelet at a strong 90° angle. While bending, the beads will pull down into the bracelet, but don't panic—they will bounce back to where they need to be when the pliers are removed. Align the wires properly and retape the bundle about ³/₄″ (1.9 cm) from the beads. Use a ready piece of 5″ (12.5 cm) wrap wire and begin to wrap the bundle immediately after the bead wires are inserted back into the bundle. Wrap toward the center five times to show (**Figures 7a and 7b**).

NOTE: Although the design was basically planned, upon adding the little negatives spaces required, the wrap marks on the back/inside of the bracelet bundle might change a bit. Ignore these visual changes and continue as directed.

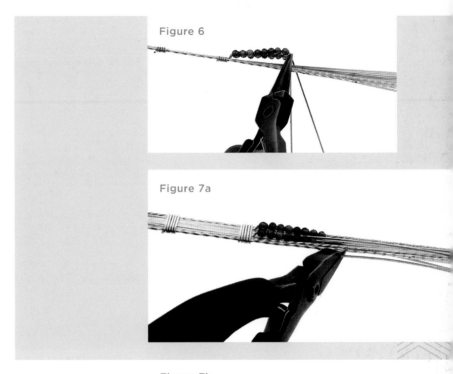

Figure 6

Figure 7a

Figure 7b

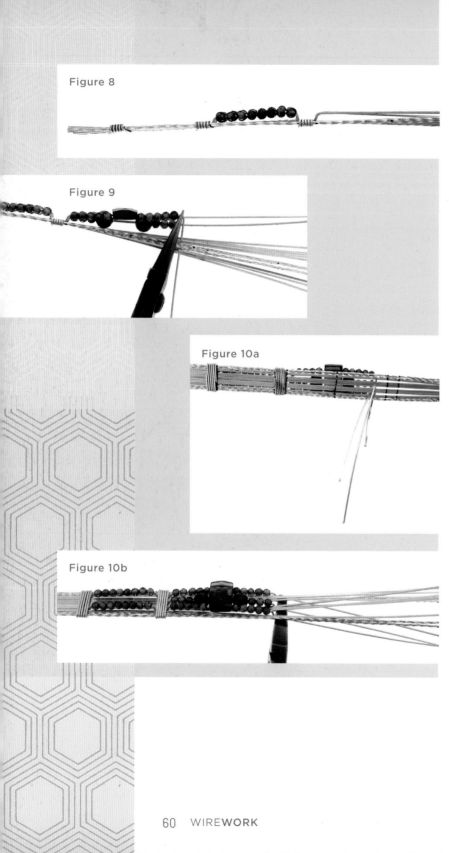

Figure 8

Figure 9

Figure 10a

Figure 10b

8

Immediately after this set of wraps, repeat Steps 4 and 5 using all three bead wires (Figure 8).

9

As this is the main focus of the bracelet, be sure to use the beads planned for the center. To make this example, use the center wire to string three 4mm CZ rounds and one 8mm CZ round. Use one outside wire to string five 4mm CZ rounds, one hole of the focal bead, and five 4mm CZ rounds. Repeat with the other outside wire. Use the center wire to string one 8mm CZ round and three 4mm CZ rounds.

10

Repeat Step 6, omitting the bead stringing. At this center point, when planning the bend to bring the bead wires back down into the bracelet bundle, it is very important to leave about 1 mm of negative space. (If using taller beads leave about 2 mm. As mentioned before, when the bracelet is shaped, the beads need this space to be able to move with the curve, not chip or break, or pull down into the bracelet base when it is finished.) When bending the bead wires, do not worry about where they are placed, as this can cause unnecessary damage to the wires as tools are repositioned and may be held too tightly (Figure 9).

11

Turn the bracelet bundle to the back/outside to see where the bead wires need to be positioned by the spaces shown. Gently reposition the bead wires and use flat-nose pliers to make the bend that returns these wires into the main bundle as in Step 7 (Figures 10a and 10b).

12

Make sure the wires are all aligned properly and retape. Immediately after the inserted bead wires, use a 5″ (12.5 cm) wire to wrap toward the end five times to show. NOTE: On the sample shown, the marks on the back/inside of the bracelet are no longer where they began. Ignore and continue with the directions **(Figure 11)**.

13

Remove the tape and create the final bead platforms, repeating Steps 4 to 7. Realign the wires and retape. Use a 5″ (12.5 cm) piece of wire to wrap toward the end five times to show. Move to the final mark, 1/2″ (1.2 cm) in from the end, and working from the mark toward the center, wrap five times to show. Remember to begin and end this wrap two wires shy of the edge **(Figure 12)**.

14

Follow the Shaping a Wire Bracelet procedure on page 40 in the Bracelet Basics section to shape the bracelet by hand. With the back/inside of the bracelet bundle facing up, use a pair of split-ring openers placed three wires in on the new center of the bundle (determined by looking at the center bead) and pull into a chevron shape **(Figure 13)**. Define the chevron shape by turning the bracelet bundle to face the front/top and repeating with the split-ring opener pull so the center bead is framed within the opening made **(Figure 14)**.

15

Follow the Hook-and-Eye Clasp procedure and the Finishing a Multi-Wire Bracelet procedure on pages 42–43 in the Bracelet Basics section to finish the bracelet ends, make the connection loops that will contain the clasp, and make and connect the hook-and-eye clasp.

Figure 11

Figure 12

Figure 13

Figure 14

chapter four

EARRINGS

For most women, earrings are the impulse buy, second only to rings. They can be quick, easy, and fun to make. Past fashion ruled that conservative earring styles were to be worn during the day, while large, flashy designs were reserved for evening attire. Today, anything goes!

EARRING BASICS

Creating a matching set of left and right earrings is easy when you make the two side by side and mirror each move and bend respectively. To be able to repeat a special design, use a piece of graph paper to draw the desired shape first, then bend the wire to match the shape. When searching for a matching set of faceted gemstones, be concerned with the size and shape of the stone's circumference, not the carat weight.

TIP

When purchasing gemstones, do not purchase by the carat weight, as some stones, such as corundum (sapphires), are very heavy compared to topaz. Instead, buy stones according to their size and shape.

angel chandelier EARRINGS

These charming earrings are made entirely of twisted wire, which gives them a diamond-cut look and adds sparkle to the center rosettes. Jewelry like this, made entirely of twisted wires, holds together because it is wrapped with a square half-hard wire. To be able to create matching left and right earrings, make them both at the same time. Or try making a single "angel" as a pendant for a special little girl.

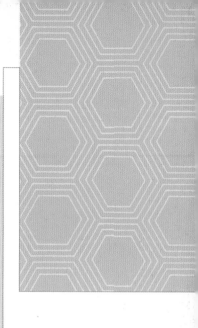

materials

34" (86.4 cm) of 22-gauge square half-hard wire

1 pair of ear wires

12 gold-filled 3mm round beads

16 faceted 5mm round beads

10 faceted 6x9mm oval beads

(Note: If larger/longer beads are chosen, the wire lengths will need to be longer.)

Finished Size: 1¼" × 2" (3.25 × 5 cm)

tools

Ruler

Flat-nose pliers

Pin vise

Chain-nose pliers

Fine round-nose pliers

Wire cutters

1

For each earring, straighten, clean, measure, and cut one 15" (8.1cm) piece of 22-gauge wire. Twist the entire length of the wire. Cut the wire into five 3" (7.5 cm) pieces.

2

Bundle the five wires together with one flush end and tape near each end. Measure 1" (2.5 cm) down from the flush end and mark across the bundle. Use 2" (5 cm) of un-twisted wire and the tip of flat-nose pliers to make a hook ⁵⁄₈" (1.5 cm) from the end of the 2" (5 cm) wire. From the 1" (2.5 cm) mark, wrap down the length of the bundle three times to show. Use a pin vise to twist the ⁵⁄₈" (1.5 cm) end and rosette down to place on top of the wraps. (In traditional wire jewelry designs, a rosette is a spiral that has been very tightly made, using square wire that has or has not been twisted. The twisted wire gives a diamond-cut effect to the spiral, thus a "rosette" is born.) To mirror the image for the other earring, be sure to start the wrap in the opposite direction. This is now the front of the earring **(Figure 1)**.

Figure 1

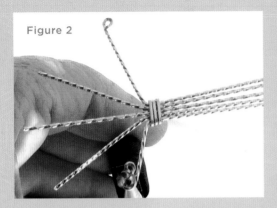

Figure 2

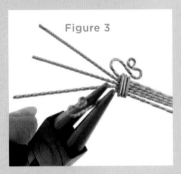

Figure 3

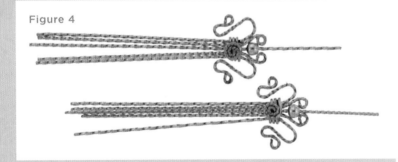

Figure 4

Remove the tape and fan out the shorter top wires. To create the wings, place the tip of the chain-nose pliers on the very end of the outermost wire (the one just above the wraps) and make a small loop, rolling down toward the "body" of the angel. Place the tip of the round-nose pliers immediately above the loop just made and roll the wire back toward the top of the bundle (**Figure 2**). Place the round-nose pliers on the same wire so that the wire is midway up the pliers' jaw, just above where the small loop is positioned, and roll down toward the body (**Figure 3**). Repeat procedure on the opposite side to create a pair of "wings."

On the next (now outer) wire, measure from the wrap up and trim to $3/8''$ (.9 cm) long. Use the tips of the chain-nose pliers to make a tiny loop heading toward the center wire. Repeat on the opposite side. Use the center wire to string one 3mm round bead, or "head." Roll the top of the wing loops toward the center wire, locking the head into place (**Figure 4**).

5

Fan the bottom "gown" wires out. Working from the outer sides toward the center, use the first wires to string one 3mm round, one 5mm round, and one 6x9mm oval (or assorted other beads chosen to represent the angel's gown). Immediately after the last bead, use flat-nose pliers to make a 90° angle away from the center wire. Trim the wire end to $1/2''$ (1.2 cm) and form a rosette toward the center, ending beneath the last bead. On the second wires, string one 3mm round, two 5mm rounds, and one 6x9mm oval. Repeat using the center wire **(Figure 5)**.

6

Use chain-nose pliers to hold a space immediately above the "head" bead and bend the center wire 90° to the right over the top jaw of the pliers (on other earring, bend to the left). Form a wrapped loop. Attach one ear wire to each wrapped loop **(Figure 6)**.

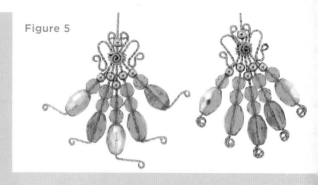

Figure 5

Figure 6

Design variation using pink beads and adding length and motion to the gown with head-pin drops.

gem drop EARRINGS

In addition to creating a gorgeous pair of earrings, this project is designed to focus on mixing wire gauges to frame a smaller gemstone (using minimal wire on the stone) and to show how to add embellishments, such as chain, in a compact manner. Although the sample design is made using a specific stone size and shape, it can easily be adapted to many other sizes/shapes.

materials

18" (45.8 cm) of 22-gauge square half-hard wire

12" (30.5 cm) of 24-gauge square half-hard wire

10" (25.5 cm) of 21-gauge half round half-hard wire

11" of fine chain

2 pear-shaped 9x14mm stones

1 pair of ear wires

Finished Size: 2¼" (5.8 cm)

tools

Wire cutters

Pin vise

Round-nose pliers

Medium and fine chain-nose pliers

Flat-nose pliers

Ruler

Tape

Fine-point marker

1

Straighten, clean, measure, and cut all of the necessary wires and chain. Cut the 22-gauge wire into six 3" (7.5 cm) pieces. Cut the 24-gauge wire into four 3" (7.5 cm) pieces. Cut the 21-gauge wire into two 5" (12.5 cm) pieces. Cut the chain into two 2¼" (5.6 cm) pieces and two 2³/₄" (7 cm) pieces.

2

Individually twist two pieces of 22-gauge wire. Make a bundle of wires for each earring, placing the gauges as follows: 24, 22 twisted, 24, 22, and 22, tape with one flush end. Measure the center of each bundle at 1½" (3.7 cm) and mark. Measure ⅛" (.3 cm) to each side of the center and mark again. Using one piece of 21-gauge half-round wire for each earring, wrap the entire center of each bundle. Reserve remaining half-round wire for later **(Figure 1)**.

3

Use an item just smaller than the stone, such as the double-barrel pliers, to make a U shape at the center of each bundle **(Figure 2)**.

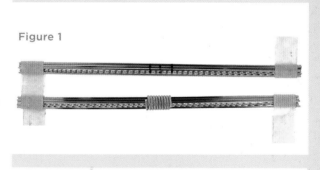

Figure 1

Figure 2

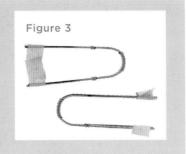
Figure 3

Figure 4

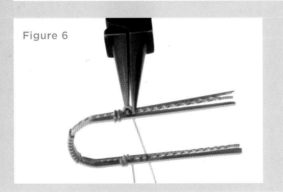
Figure 5

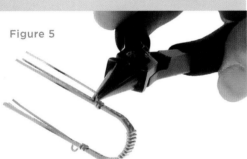
Figure 6

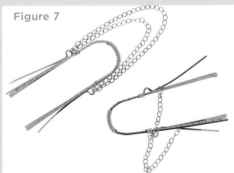
Figure 7

4

Measure $7/16''$ (1.1 cm) up from the side of each wrap and mark on the edge of each shape. Use the remaining half-round wire to add two full wraps on each side, working from these marks up **(Figure 3)**.

5

Remove all of the tape. Use flat-nose pliers to hold onto the wrap wire while bending each center (24-gauge) wire out at a 90° angle **(Figure 4)**.

6

Use the tips of fine chain-nose pliers to form two-thirds of a small box shape on each of these center wires **(Figures 5 and 6)**. (See page 100, Drop Necklace Base Design.)

7

Insert one end of one $2^1/4''$ (5.6 cm) chain onto each of the 24-gauge wires with the box shapes. Repeat with the longer chain, creating the festoons **(Figure 7)**.

8

Fit the stone into the setting, making sure that the second wire in from the front of the stone is the twisted one. Use flat-nose pliers to bend and hold the wires above the stone. Tape into place (**Figure 8**).

9

Use 2″ (5 cm) of 22-gauge wire to begin a wrap at the bend above the stone and wrap up three times to show, making sure the wire ends are toward the back of each earring and trim flush (**Figure 9**).

10

Working on the front of an earring first, use medium chain-nose pliers to grasp the very top wire immediately next to the bottom/center wrap and make one smooth bend over and toward the stone. Repeat on the other side of the center and again on the other earring (**Figure 10**). Resist the urge to use needle-nose pliers for this move, as more than likely the wire will snap due to the sharpness of the jaw.

11

Using flat-nose pliers to grasp the wire on the back of each earring, repeat Step 9 (**Figure 11**).

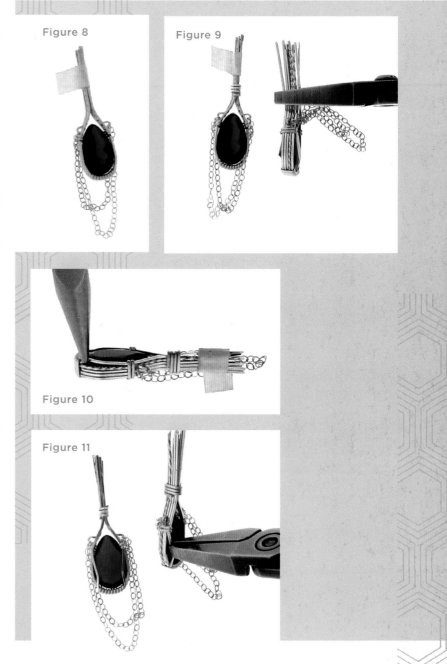

Figure 8

Figure 9

Figure 10

Figure 11

Figure 12

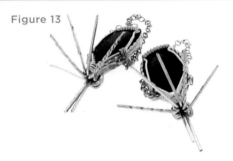

Figure 13

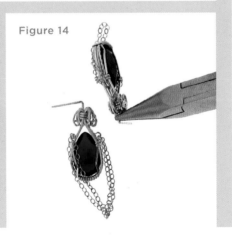

Figure 14

12

12

Working on the back of the earrings, bend two wires down on one side and one on the other (mirror these on the other earring). Trim each wire so that it is just a bit longer than the wrap it is going over. Use chain-nose pliers to put a slight curve into each end and then flat-nose pliers to push them into place, ending alongside the wrapped top (**Figure 12**). (Similar to finishing the center cut wires of the Chevron Bracelet Base, page 47.)

13

Working on the front of the earrings, fan out the five wires in the front, trim the outer four to $3/8''$ (1 cm) and the front center wire to $1/2''$ (1.2 cm) (**Figure 13**).

14

Use chain-nose pliers to make a tiny loop at the end of each of the $3/8''$ (1 cm) wires, heading down. Use flat-nose pliers to slightly roll each loop down toward the top wrap, producing a crown effect. Make a rosette with the $1/2''$ (1.2 cm) front wire and place it directly on the top wrap. Use medium chain-nose pliers to hold a space on the last 22-gauge wire and use fingers to bend the wires' end over the chain-nose jaw, 90° to one side, (mirror on the other earring) (**Figure 14**).

15

Using round-nose pliers, make a simple loop at the top corner of the 22-gauge wire, forming the wire completely around the jaw (Figure 15).

16

Wrap the tail of the loop around the back of the loop stem and crimp it tightly with flat-nose pliers. Trim flush (Figure 16).

17

Straighten the loops and attach ear wires (Figure 17).

Figure 15

Figure 16

Figure 17

sparkle EARRINGS

Basic and sweet, these earrings were designed to show one of the ways to properly set and lock a stone into a snap-set finding. Snap-set heads are one of my favorite findings because I love to be able to use a tiny stone, such as a 3mm or 4mm round, to accent a particular design. Try stacking a 5mm round above a 6mm, replacing the chain segments with head-pin drops, adding head-pin drops to the bottom of the chain segments, or eliminating the chain altogether—this design has unlimited potential!

materials

14" (35.6 cm) of 22-gauge square half-hard wire

2 round 8mm snap-set heads

2 round 8mm faceted stones

4 silver 2mm rounds

6 textured 4mm rounds

2³/₄" (6.9 cm) of fine chain

1 pair of ear wires

Finished Size: 2½" (5.8 cm) long

tools

Flat-nose pliers

Fine chain-nose pliers

Round-nose pliers

Cutters

Tape

Double-barrel pliers

Ruler

Fine-point marker

Pin vise

DESIGN NOTE

When using smaller snap-set heads, a 22-gauge wire many not fit under the stone, try using a 24-gauge instead. Square wire is used, as round wire has a tendency to slip when least desired and cannot be twisted.

1

Prepare the snap-set heads. Occasionally the prongs on these heads are bent during packaging, shipping, etc. Use flat-nose pliers on the sides of the prongs to gently push them back into place **(Figure 1).**

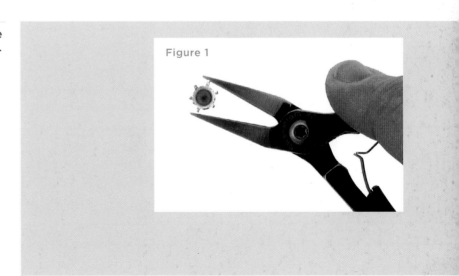

Figure 1

Figure 2

Figure 3

Figure 4

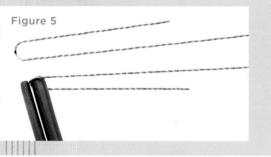

Figure 5

Figure 6

2

Set the stones. Use a wide tape to make two round segments, with the sticky side facing out. Put one of these tape rounds on a solid, flat surface and place the stone, crown/table side down, pavilion up, onto the tape. Put the other tape round onto an index finger and put the snap-set finding on it (Figure 2). Center the finding over the stone and press down, quickly and firmly (Figure 3). The stone will "snap" into the setting. Repeat with the second stone.

3

Check each stone in its setting to make sure all of the prongs are snuggly over the edge/girdle of the stone. If any of the prongs are not where they need to be, place the tip of fine chain-nose pliers under the stone and gently push it up into the prong (Figure 4).

4

Twist 7" (18.9 cm) of wire. Measure 2" (5 cm) down from one end of the wire and mark. Choose a shaping item or tool that is just a bit smaller than the circumference of the stone's edge/girdle, such as a smaller pair of double-barrel pliers. Center the shaping item/tool on the 2" (5 cm) mark and bend the wire to form a U shape. Repeat for the second earring (Figure 5).

5

Use one end of one U-shaped wire to string ³⁄₈" (1 cm) of chain, one 2mm bead, ¹⁄₂" (1.2 cm) of chain, one 2mm bead, and ³⁄₈" (1 cm) of chain. Repeat for the second earring (Figure 6).

6

Use one U-shaped wire and carefully thread each end through one snap-set, making sure the wire passes under the stone and under the center prong on each side. Gently work the wires up through the finding until the beaded/chain segment is just under the bottom of the stone. Repeat for the second earring **(Figure 7)**.

7

Use the longer wire of one U shape to wrap over the top of the finding, crossing in front of the shorter wire and down completely around the stone, making sure it is snug and just under the prongs/girdle and that the wire wraps in front of the chain/bead segment **(Figures 8 and 9)**. When this longer wire meets the shorter wire again at the top, straighten the shorter wire and wrap the longer one around it twice, from front to back, ending with this wire at a 90° angle to the earring **(Figure 10)**. Repeat for the second earring, wrapping in the opposite direction **(Figure 11)**.

8

Place a shaping tool against the shorter stem just above the wrap and bend the longer wire over the tool at a 90° angle, crossing over the front of the shorter wire. Repeat for the second earring, wrapping in the opposite direction. NOTE: One of the barrel pliers is used here, however any shape may be chosen. For example, the outside of V-making pliers would work well when using bicone beads **(Figure 12)**.

Figure 7

Figure 8

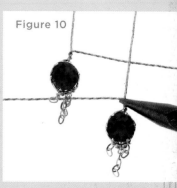

Figure 9

Figure 10

Figure 11

Figure 12

Figure 13

Figure 14

Figure 15

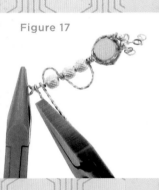

Figure 15

Figure 16

Figure 17

Figure 18

9

Use the straight wire to string two 4mm rounds. Then wrap the longer curved wire around and behind the shorter wire one full time immediately above the beads. Repeat for the second earring (**Figure 13**).

10

Place a slightly smaller shaping tool against the bead stem immediately above the wrap just made and repeat Step 8. Use the straight wire to string one 4mm round and repeat Step 9 (**Figures 14 and 15**).

11

Place the tips of chain-nose pliers onto the bead stem immediately after the wrapped longer wire and hold the space while using fingers to bend the bead stem over the pliers to the side at a 90° angle (**Figure 16**). Place round-nose pliers on the top of the corner just made and form a loop (**Figure 17**). Hold the loop with one pair of pliers while using another to wrap it in. Repeat for the second earring, wrapping in the opposite direction (**Figure 18**).

12

Trim the remaining longer wire end to $3/8''$ (1 cm). Use fine chain-nose pliers to start and flat-nose pliers to rosette this wire, placing it on top of the stem wraps **(Figure 19)**. Repeat for the second earring. Attach one ear wire to each earring **(Figure 20)**.

Figure 19

Figure 20

Design variation without chain and using fewer accent beads.

chapter five

PENDANTS AND NECKLACES

What a great way to show off a beautiful stone—make a pendant! If the stone is plain, dress it up by adding crystals or other beads, and/or wire embellishments. If a stone is gorgeous, then I believe in "celebrating the stone" and make as simple a setting as possible. A necklace can be a single pendant on a wire collar or chain, or it can be a very elaborate collaboration of pendant variations, adorned with chains, head-pin charms, and beads. The choice is yours.

BAILS

A bail should be large enough to accommodate a large spring clasp, as this is the type of clasp most folks have on their chains. If the bail is long and thin, it can be modified with careful use of round-nose pliers and lengthened to fit over an Omega clasp or rounded to fit a heavy rope chain. In rare cases, you may have to make an alternative connection, such as the one found in the "Fish" design on page 86. A nice bail may have its wires slightly separated by using a dull blade but not pulled apart like funky rabbit ears. When using dead-soft wire, please remember that it needs to be twisted before making a bail, to strengthen the wire first.

DON'T BE SHY WITH WIRE

One of the biggest challenges I find is that folks tend to skimp on the amount of wires used to make a pendant frame. In these cases, the students have had major issues with being able to properly grasp the wire they wish to pull over the stone because the frame doesn't come all the way to the top of the girdle or edge of the stone being set. Reaching down to get this wire with either flat-nose or chain-nose pliers and then pulling it over the stone usually causes the wrap wire next to the wire being pulled to unwrap partway, causing a sloppy look. This will also cause the top wire pulls to be uneven on the stone, throwing off what symmetry was desired.

TIP

Keep a segment of chain and a hand mirror at your work space. Whenever a pendant is finished, hang it from the chain and put it up to your own neck to see how it will lie.

mixed wire cabochon fish
PENDANT

The fish pattern below is just an example of how to play with mixing dead-soft and half-hard wire tempers. The main frame shape is held stable by using half-hard wire, while the flowing tail is sculpted using dead-soft. Unlike the other designs in this book, this one is meant to show off the wire design, instead of the stone. Of course, using a stone that has a shape and/or color pattern that resembles an animal or such can bring excellent visual results to the finished piece. Additional movement and color can be added by threading beads or crystals onto the fins and tail, too!

materials

21- or 22-gauge square half-hard wire—3 pieces measured from the formula of circumference of the stone plus 4″ (10 cm)

2″ (5 cm) of 21- or 22-gauge square half-hard wire for the end wrap

21- or 22-gauge square dead-soft wire—2 or 3 pieces measured from the formula of circumference of stone plus 4″ or 6″ (10 or 15 cm). (The length chosen depends on how elaborate the sculpted section will be. The amount needed equals as many wires as it takes to cover the side of the cabochon plus two.)

12″ (30.2 cm) of 20-gauge half-round half-hard wire for the side wrap wires

3″ (7.5 cm) of 21-gauge #8 spring-hard wire

22x30mm black onyx oval cabochon or cabochon of choice

Note: To differentiate, this project uses square silver half-hard and square gold-filled dead-soft wires.

Finished Size: 2¼″ × 2″ (5.7 × 5.5 cm)

tools

Wire cutters

Ruler

Tape

Marker

Flat-nose pliers

Pin vise

Shaping tool

Chain-nose pliers

3-stepped pliers

Figure 1

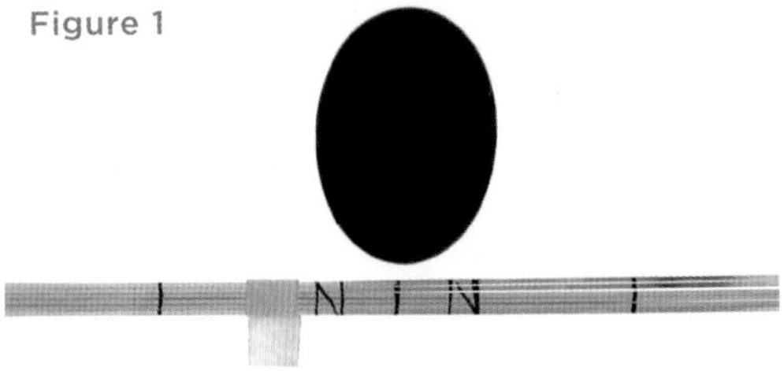

Figure 2

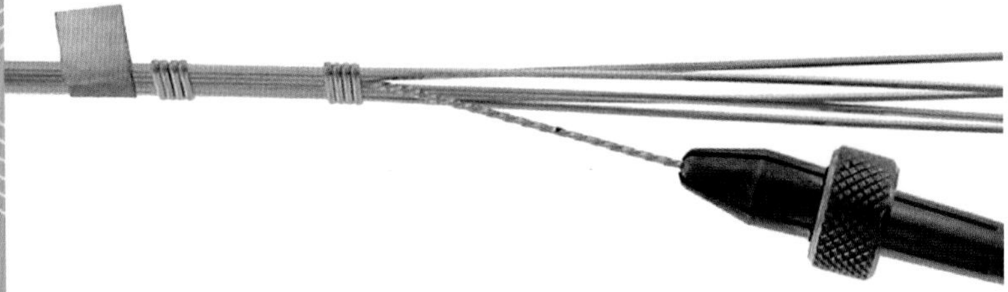

Figure 3

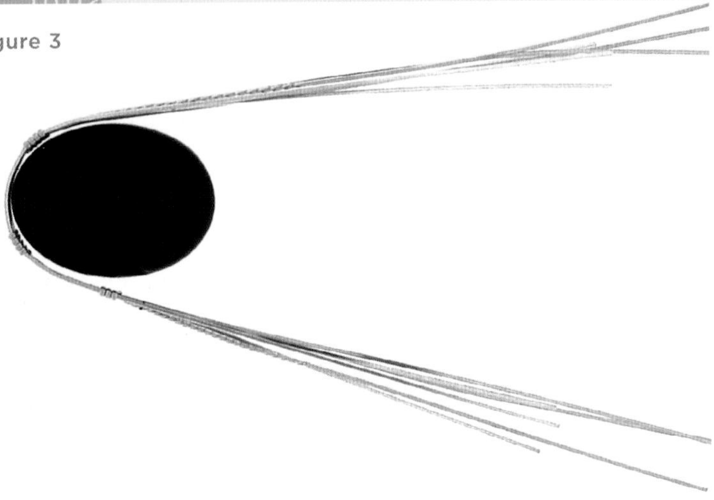

MIXED-WIRE CABOCHON FISH PENDANT

1

Straighten, clean, measure, and cut all of the 21/22-gauge wires. Bundle the wires together, with two half-hard lengths on one side and one half-hard length on the other, centering all of the dead-soft wires in the middle of the bundle. Tape in two places: near each end of the bundle and just off-center. Mark each taped end L and R. Find and mark the center of the bundle. Place this center mark on any whole number and measure $1/2''$ (1.2 cm) to either side and mark again. From each of these new marks, measure $1/8''$ (.3 cm) toward each end and mark. With the back of the bundle facing up, on the R end of the bundle, measure $3/4''$ (1.9 cm) from the $1/8''$ (.3 cm) mark just made, toward the R end of the wires, and mark. On the L end of the bundle, measure $1/2''$ (1.2 cm) from the $1/8''$ (.3 cm) mark just made, and mark **(Figure 1)**.

2

Cut the 20-gauge wire into two 6" (15 cm) pieces. Use flat-nose pliers and one piece of 20-gauge wire to wrap the bundle at the $1/8''$ (.3 cm) marks four times to show, working away from the center on each side. On the L end wrap from the last mark made toward the end, three times to show. Remove all tape. On the R end, lift the center dead-soft wire toward the front of the bundle and use a pin vise to twist a $1^1/2''$ (3.7 cm) segment immediately after the wrap. On the L end, lift the center dead-soft wire toward the front and twist a $3/4''$ (1.9 cm) segment **(Figure 2)**.

NOTE: The R end of the bundle will become the top of the fish outline and the L end, the bottom, and the side of the bundle with two half-hard wires being the top of the cabochon. Use a shaping tool or found item to curve the bundle into the shape of the face of the fish (Figure 3).

3

Use the twisted center wire on the top of the frame to create the top fin of the fish. Use the twisted wire on the bottom center to make the bottom fin. Remember, this is your design and can be realistic . . . or not! Return the twisted wires to their positions in the bundle and retape. Use half-round wire to secure each of the fins immediately after their return to the bundle, wrapping three times to show toward the ends.

NOTE: Keep in mind when shaping the top fin that the bail will be attached to it, and adjustments can be made later (Figure 4).

4

Continue shaping the fish frame around the cabochon. Crisscross the bundle ends near the "tail" and mark (Figure 5). Remove all tape. At these marks, use flat-nose pliers to bend each bundle end out at a 45° angle. Tape frame together (Figure 6).

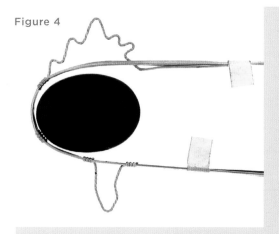

Figure 4

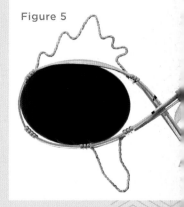

Figure 5

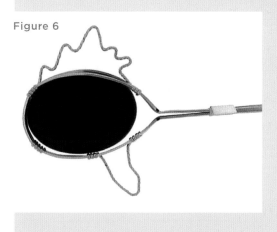

Figure 6

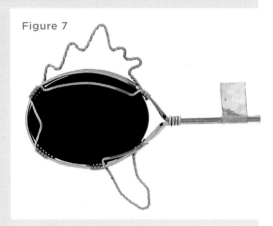

Figure 7

5

Use the remaining 2″ (5 cm) of 20-gauge wire to wrap the frame together at the base of the tail, placing the wire hook at the bottom of the frame heading toward the back of the pendant. Wrap two times to show. Do not cut the wrap wire. Use flat-nose pliers to make the pulls on the back and chain-nose pliers on the front, locking the stone into the frame. (Refer to page 51 for detailed directions.) Finish wrapping the frame for a total of four times to show. Trim the wrap wire on the side **(Figure 7)**.

6

Remove the tape and use fingers and/or tools to trim, twist, spiral, sculpt, and swirl the "tail" wires, remembering to put a small full curl at each end **(Figure 8)**.

7

Use the largest barrel on 3-step pliers and the spring-hard wire to make a 3-turned spring/coil. Attach the spring coil to the top fin **(Figure 9)**.

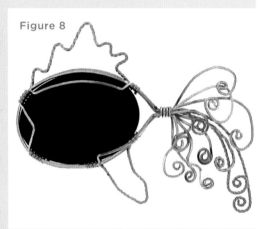

Figure 8

Figure 9

TIP

Give your fish personality and add to the design by making the front pulls different lengths and shapes. Remember to begin at the center and work toward each end.

cabochons in geometric pendant

Sherrie Lingerfelt combined techniques from the *Ornate Cabochon Topping pattern* (page 49) with her love of geometry to design this pendant.

Finished size: 1″ x 2⅛″ (2.5 x 5.4 cm)

sea treasure glass and wire pendant

To set her glass designs, Lindi Lou Schneck utilizes ideas from the *Mixed-Wire Fish Pendant.*

Finished size: 1¾″ x 2″ (4.4 x 5.1 cm)

orbit prong gemstone
PENDANT

The goal of many wire-jewelry enthusiasts is to make beautiful crisp prongs from wire. Making them correctly and being able to hold a stone properly is not as difficult as many would have you believe. This design, where the depth of the pavilion is not an issue, is the perfect first step in learning to handcraft wire prongs. As your skills and confidence grow and you move on to larger stones, adjust the length of the base wire as necessary.

materials

33$\frac{1}{2}$" (85 cm) of 20-, 21-, or 22-gauge square half-hard wire (choose wire gauge according to the stone size)

12x16mm cut stone or stone of choice (it's best to begin with a square or rectangular shape and progress to an oval, pear, or round stone).

tools

Wire cutters

Tape

Ruler

Flat-nose pliers

Medium chain-nose pliers

Ring mandrel (or other round shaping tool)

Thin dull blade

Pin vice

3-stepped round pliers

Finished Size: 1$\frac{1}{16}$" × 1$\frac{1}{4}$" (2.5 × 3 cm)

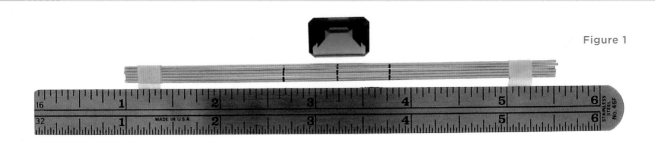

Figure 1

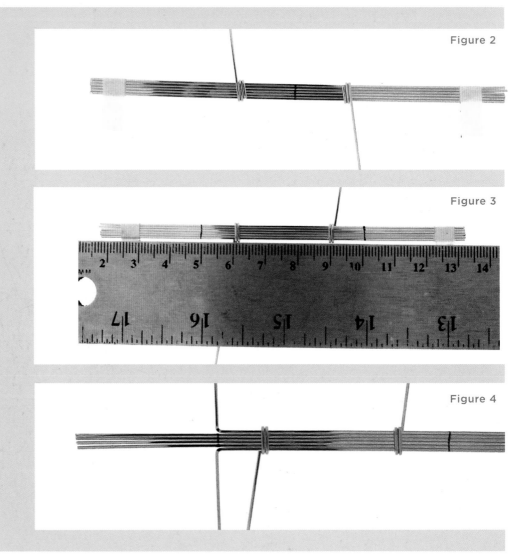

Figure 2

Figure 3

Figure 4

ORBIT PRONG GEMSTONE PENDANT

1

Straighten, clean, measure, and cut all of the necessary wires. Cut the wire into six $4^1/2''$ (11.3 cm) pieces and two $3^1/4''$ (8.1 cm) pieces. Bundle the six $4^1/2''$ (11.3 cm) wires together with one flush end and tape near each end. Measure and mark the center of the bundle. Measure the height and width of the stone, add the two measurements together, and divide in half. This is the distance to measure and mark on each side of the center mark. For example, 16mm x 12mm stone = 28mm divided by 2 = 14mm, which is then marked to each side of the center mark **(Figure 1)**.

2

Use one $3^1/4''$ (8.1 cm) wire to begin a wrap at one of the side marks, across the entire bundle. Working away from the center, make two full wraps to show on front. Do not cut this wrap wire. Use the other $3^1/4''$ (8.1 cm) wire to begin a wrap at the other side mark, starting it in the opposite direction of the first and working away from the center. Make two full wraps to show and stop. Do not cut this wire **(Figure 2)**.

3

On the front of the pendant bundle (the side currently without marks), measure $3/8''$ (1 cm) from the outer edge of the wrap wire, away from the center, and mark one thin straight line across entire bundle **(Figure 3)**.

4

Working with one end of the wire bundle, place flat-nose pliers on one of the outer wires immediately above the marks just made and bend out at a sharp 90° angle. Repeat using the other outer wire of the same end. Make sure the two bends are totally equal **(Figure 4)**. These bent wires will now be referred to as the prong wires.

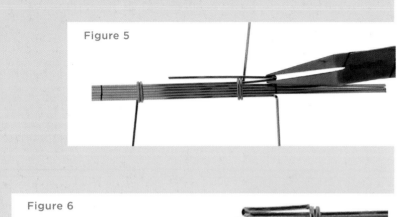

Figure 5

Figure 6

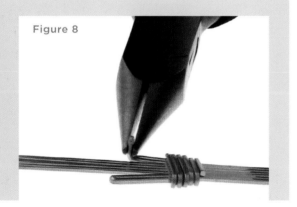

Figure 7

Figure 8

Fold one prong wire back against itself and use flat-nose pliers to firmly crimp the fold (**Figure 5**). Repeat using the other prong wire.

Trim prong wire ends so they sit immediately next to the pendant bundle, above the wraps (**Figure 6**).

Use the wrap wire to wrap the prong wire into the main bundle, adding three complete wraps for a total of five wraps to show on the front. Trim wrap wire flush with main bundle (**Figure 7**).

Repeat Steps 4 to 7, beginning on the other end of the wire bundle so there are a total of four prong wires completed.

Gently fan each of the four prongs toward the sides, slightly away from the main bundle. Hold the pendant bundle so the back is facing you (where wrap ends are). Place the tip of medium chain-nose pliers on the prong end and bend toward the back at sharp 90° angle. Repeat for the three remaining prongs (**Figure 8**). NOTE: Prong length should be approximately 2 mm long.

10

Place the tip of the chain-nose pliers immediately under the angle just formed and bend 90° in the opposite direction, making an L shape on top of the prong wire. Repeat for the three remaining prongs. Check the bends to make sure all four prong wires match. If needed, make small adjustments, being careful to adjust just a little bit at a time (Figure 9).

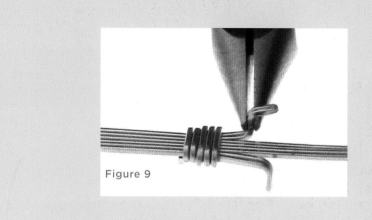

Figure 9

11

Place the tips of the chain-nose pliers near the base of one newly formed prong and bend the prong slightly toward the back/inside of the pendant bundle, where the wraps end (Figure 10).

Figure 10

12

Use a ring mandrel or other shaping item to form a U shape with the bundle by eyeballing the size of the stone, then placing the back of the pendant bundle (where the wrap wires end) against the mandrel and pressing simultaneously on the wraps, taking care to not disturb the prongs. NOTE: Due to the temper of half-hard wire, the shaping item chosen needs to be just a bit smaller than the stone size (Figure 11).

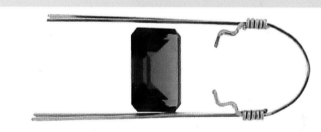

Figure 11

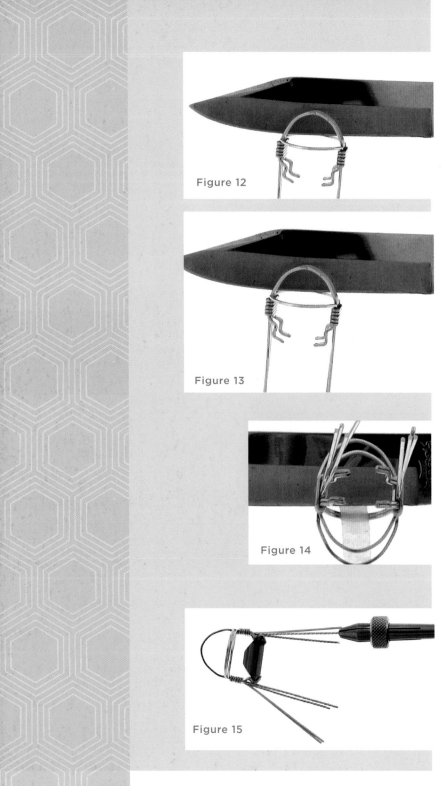

Figure 12

Figure 13

Figure 14

Figure 15

13

Slide the stone into the prongs and check for a proper fit. Make any necessary adjustments to the prongs, moving them just a little at a time, until stone fits snuggly into the prongs. Remove the stone. Carefully place a thin dull blade between the first and second wires of one side of the U shape and bend the first curved wire out so that it is at a 90° angle to the pendant bundle. Repeat on the other side of the U shape **(Figure 12)**.

14

On the outside of the pendant shape, mark the curved wires immediately after the wrap wires on each end. Gently pull the remaining curved wires out of the wraps until they are 3mm longer on each end, by checking the mark made after wraps **(Figure 13)**.

15

Repeat Step 13, placing the blade between the second and third wires and bending the second wires so that they are next to the first wires bent. These second rings will be a bit larger than the first, forming the orbit shape **(Figure 14)**.

16

Fit the stone into the prongs and make any necessary final adjustments. There are now four wires sticking out of the top and bottom, with a stone in the center. Gently form slight bends on the center two wires at each end by using your fingers to press them toward the outside of the pendant, just enough to get them out of the way for a bit. If desired, use a pin vise to individually twist each of the four outer wires (**Figure 15**).

NOTE: While completing Steps 17 to 23, please hold the stone carefully in place so as not to disturb the prong placements.

17

Use your fingers to form one of the twisted side wires up and along the side of the stone. Use chain-nose pliers to tease a curve into the end of the wire (**Figure 16**). Work this curved end around and under the prong at the opposite end of the stone from where the wire started (**Figure 17**). Pressing only on the wire being worked with, close the curved end around the prong and trim.

18

Working from the same end of the pendant, repeat Step 17 using the other twisted wire, wrapping around the opposite side of the stone, thus locking the stone into place (**Figure 18**).

19

Repeat Steps 17 and 18 on the other end of the pendant, placing each new twisted wire above the previous twisted wire, just under the girdle of the stone (**Figure 19**).

Figure 16

Figure 17

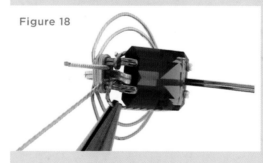

Figure 18

Figure 19

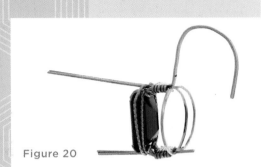

Figure 20

20

Gently bend the remaining center wires (the wires slightly bent in Step 16) back into their original straight positions. Decide which is the top and which is to be the bottom of the pendant. On the back bottom of the piece, gently pull the curved wires back through the wraps until they are about ³/₄" (1.9 cm) long on the bottom front. On the back bottom, cut the curved wires ¹/₄" (.6 cm) behind the bottom wraps. Bend the longer cut wires toward the top of the pendant (**Figure 20**). These will become the bail wires.

21

At the bottom back, bend the ¹/₄" (.6 cm) long wires up, inside, and over the wraps between the "orbit" and crimp tightly. At the bottom front, use the ³/₄" (1.9 cm) wires to either decorate with or bend each of them 90° to their corresponding side, trim to ³/₈" (1 cm) and fold up and to the inside, crimping over the bottom wires just above the five-wire wrapped segment (**Figure 21**).

Figure 21

22

Use the medium level of 3-step pliers or the smaller barrel on double-barrel pliers and the top wires to form the bail. Place the bottom jaw of the chosen tool on the bail wires 1" (2.5 cm) above the pendant and roll the bail wires toward the back of the pendant. Place flat-nose pliers on the bail wire tails and bend them up and in, forming a dip close to the front of the bail just above the top of the pendant. Use a pin vise to twist the two remaining wires sticking out the front. Crisscross these two twisted wires on top of the five-wire wrapped segment. Wrap the bottom wire twice around the bail toward the back and trim. Do not cut the other wire. Cut the wire tails of the bail to ³/₁₆" (.5 cm) long and use chain-nose pliers to roll these ends back toward the pendant, ending just under the bail wrap. Use the remaining twisted wire to form a rosette. Place the rosette on top of the bail wrap in front (**Figure 22**).

Figure 22

23

Use the dull blade to slide between the circles on each side of the pendant, raising the front one up until it forms the desired orbit height (**Figure 23**).

Figure 23

butterfly brooch/ pendant

Dottie Arnao modified the *Orbit Prong Pendant* design, to turn a marquis stone into a butterfly.

Finished size: 1" x 1⅜" (2.5 x 3.5 cm)

faerie ivory scrimshaw pendant

Mary W. Bailey's scrimshaw makes a beautiful pendant when set using techniques from the *Mixed-Wire Fish* instructions (page 83).

Finished size: 1⅛" x 2⅝" (2.9 x 6.7 cm)

drop necklace BASE DESIGN

This design is an elegant solution for making a necklace in which to show off a combination of faceted stones or cabochons. If these stones/cabochons were only attached to a chain, the chain could twist and the stones could roll and flop. The following design can be altered depending on elaborate or simple desires: make the base wider; use less or more twisted wires; add chain festoons, head-pin charms, more "attachment" boxes, and more or less rosettes. The possibilities are amazing!

materials

45" (114.4 cm) of 22-gauge square half-hard wire for the base and end wraps

12" (30.5 cm) of 20-gauge half-round half-hard wire for the center wraps

12" (30.5 cm) of chain

1 sterling silver 5x10mm lobster clasp with attached 4mm jump ring or clasp of choice (see Design Note, next page)

1 silver 1½" (3.7 cm) head pin

2 gold-filled 1.5mm round beads

1 sterling silver 2mm round bead

1 gold-filled 4mm round bead

1 sterling silver 5mm textured round bead

12½" (31.8 cm) of medium-weight chain

Finished Size (of wireworked centerpiece): 6" (15 cm)

tools

Wire cutters

Ruler

Marker

Tape

Pin vise

Medium chain-nose pliers

Fine chain-nose pliers

Round-nose pliers

Flat-nose pliers

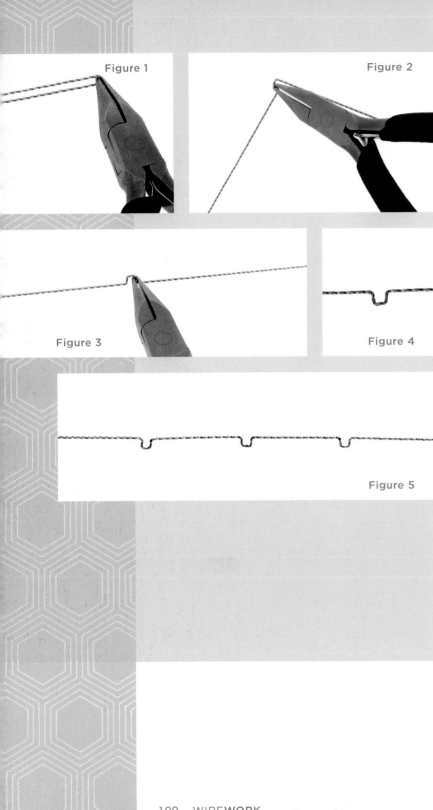

Figure 1

Figure 2

Figure 3

Figure 4

Figure 5

DESIGN NOTE

This design can be made with almost any gauge of square half-hard wire (use an appropriately gauged half-round to match). Please note that the end wraps are made with square wire to provide the strength needed to hold it all together, while the center wraps are half-round for the "look" of the design. When choosing a clasp and chain combination to use in a necklace design, choose a clasp that will fit into the links of the chosen chain so that the necklace can be worn at many different lengths. This makes the piece more versatile, which becomes more affordable to a customer!

1

Straighten and clean all needed wires. Cut the 22-gauge wire into five 7" (17.6 cm) pieces and two 5" (12.5 cm) pieces. Cut the 20-gauge wire in half. Use the pin vise or drill to individually twist two of the 7" (17.6 cm) base wires. Find and mark the center of one of the twisted 7" (17.6 cm) wires. Use chain-nose pliers to make an open box shape at this center point (Figures 1 to 4).

2

From the open box shape just made, measure 1" (2.5 cm) toward each side and mark. Form an open box shape at each mark, working away from the center. This forms the "attachment" wire. NOTE: If the attachment wire is not as straight as desired, do not panic or attempt to straighten this wire as you risk overworking or weakening it. The wire will pull into the design and straighten as it is wrapped into the design (Figure 5).

3

Place the 7″ (17.6 cm) base wires side by side, with a twisted wire at the top and center the twisted attachment wire at the bottom, with the box shapes facing out and down. Tape near the ends and where needed to keep the bundle together. Beginning at the center and then working toward each side (which helps to pull the attachment wire into position), use one piece of 20-gauge wire to wrap from each side of each attachment box five times to show, as in the diagram (**Figure 6**). Wrap wires should begin and end one wire below each edge (**Figure 7**).

4

On the front of the necklace bundle, from the last wrap at each end measure and mark $7/8$″ (2.2 cm) toward the corresponding end. Using one 5″ (12.5 cm) piece of 22-gauge wire, make a hook 1″ (2.5 cm) deep. Use this wire, with the 1″ (2.5 cm) hook on the back, to wrap two times to show toward the end and stop. Do not cut this wrap wire! From the second wrap made, measure toward the end $1/2$″ (1.2 cm) and mark the center wires. Working on the front of the bundle, remove the tape and gently separate and move the top two center wires up (remember that the attachment boxes are on the bottom), placing round-nose pliers under them just to the outside edge of the mark (**Figure 8**). On the front of the bundle, use round-nose pliers to roll these two wires back toward the wraps, continuing the roll so the wires fold/crimp toward the wraps (**Figure 9**). (To form a loop large enough for the chosen chain and to be consistent on either side, choose an appropriate size/position on the jaw of the round-nose pliers and mark this spot.) Use flat-nose pliers to press into shape (**Figure 10**).

NOTE: By making these loops on the front, uncomfortable impediments poking into the collarbone are avoided.

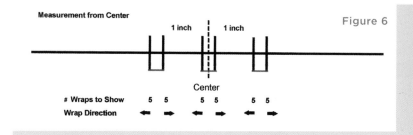

Measurement from Center
1 inch   1 inch
Center
Wraps to Show   5 5   5 5   5 5
Wrap Direction   ← →   ← →   ← →

Figure 6

Figure 7

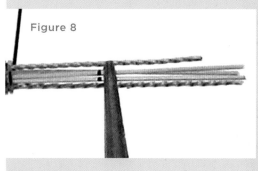

Figure 8

Figure 9

Figure 10

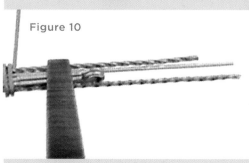

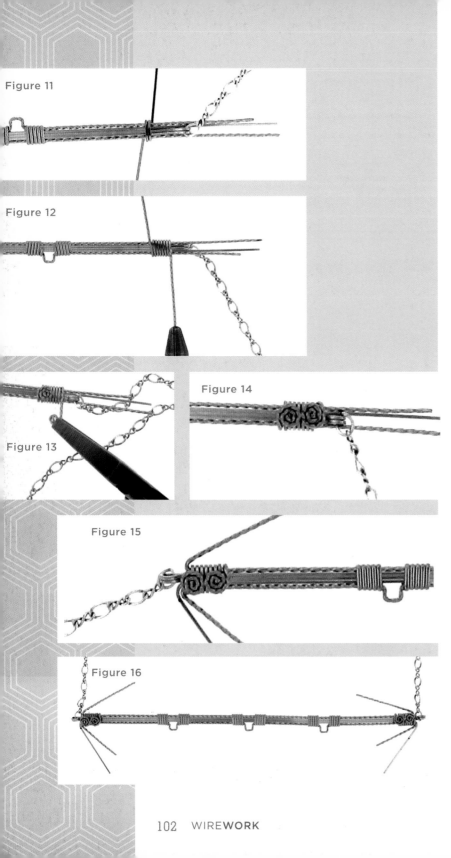

Figure 11

Figure 12

Figure 14

Figure 13

Figure 15

Figure 16

5

Cut the chain into one 5^1/$_2$" (13.8 cm) piece and one 6^1/$_2$" (16.3 cm) piece. Insert one of the pieces of chain into the loop just made (**Figure 11**). (Usually the longer length of chain goes on the left and the shorter on the right. However, for left-handed wearers or customized pieces, the positions can be reversed.) Use the wrap wire begun in Step 4 to continue wrapping, locking the loop legs into the main bundle, by adding five more wraps to show. Do not cut the wrap wire. Use a pin vise to twist each end of the wrap wire and then trim each to ^{3}/$_4$" (1.9 cm) (**Figure 12**).

6

Working on the front of the bundle, use fine chain-nose pliers to begin and then flat-nose pliers to complete rosettes with each of the twisted wrap wire ends, rolling them up and then placing them onto the main wraps on the front of the bundle (**Figures 13 and 14**).

7

Spread and gently bend the loose end wires (**Figure 15**). Repeat Steps 4 to 6 on the other end of the bundle (**Figure 16**).

8

On each side of the bundle, trim the single twisted wire at the top to $3/4''$ (1.9 cm) long. On the bottom, trim the twisted wire to $5/8''$ (1.5 cm) or $1/2''$ (1.2 cm) long and trim the untwisted wire to $3/4''$ (1.9 cm) long. Use fine chain-nose pliers to begin and flat-nose pliers to complete rosettes, placing them alongside the main bundle where desired (**Figure 17**).

9

Keeping the necklace bundle flat, hold it firmly and beginning at the center, slowly form an arch shape into the frame, working toward each side (**Figure 18**). Work it about $1/2''$ (1.2 cm) at a time, until the desired shape is attained (**Figures 19 and 20**).

10

Use the head pin and beads to make and attach a charm to the longer chain. Attach the clasp to the shorter chain (**Figure 21**).

11

Lay the necklace on a flat surface and carefully make any final adjustments. It is now ready to be finished by adding the desired stones, cabochons, and/or charms to the attachment boxes (**Figure 22**). Please see page 104 for ideas.

Figure 17

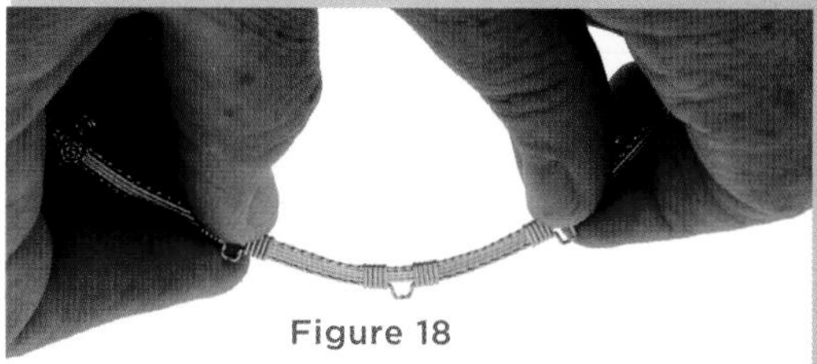

Figure 18

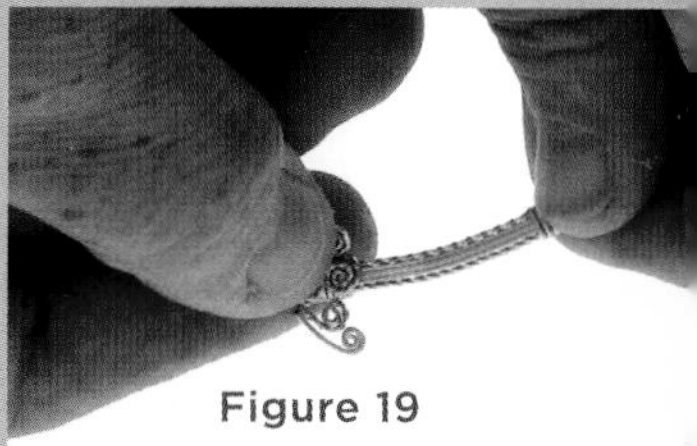

Figure 19

Figure 20

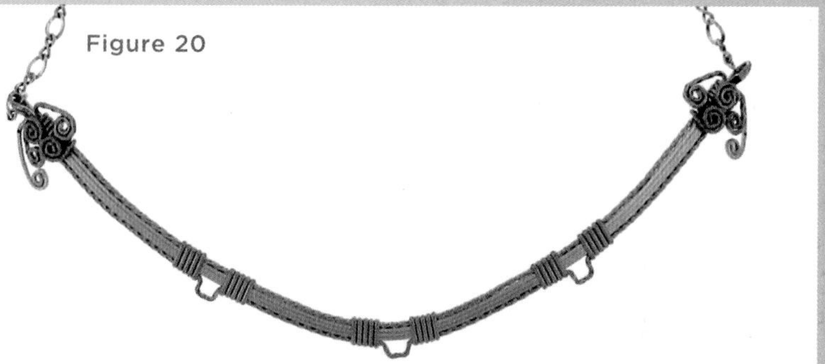

Figure 21

Figure 22

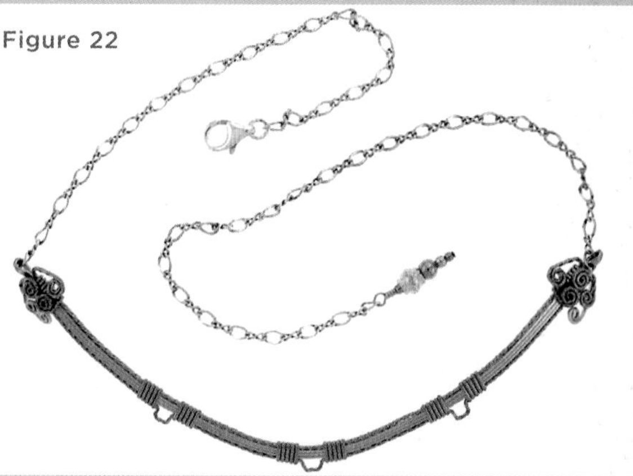

gemstone/cabochon
DROP FOR ATTACHMENT

Add interest and texture to the Drop Necklace base design by border- or frame-wrapping cabochons and/or faceted gemstones. Create unusual combinations by using a variety of gemstones and cabochons of different shapes, sizes, and styles. Further elaborations can include chains, beads, and head-pin charms.

materials

22- or 24-gauge (or a combination of the two gauges) square half-hard wire for the frame

36" to 72" (91.5 to 182.9 cm) of 20- or 21-gauge half-round half-hard wire for the Wrap Wire (12" to 24" [30.5 to 61 cm] per drop)

6" (15 cm) of 22- and/or 24-gauge (same gauge as the frame wire) square half-hard wire for the top wrap (2" [5 cm] per drop)

2 Uvarovite Garnet Drusy 10x15mm inverted triangle cabochons (or cabochons of choice)

1 Mount Saint Helens Emerald 10x15mm cut stone (or stone of choice)

Finished Size: cabochons are ⁷⁄₁₆" × 1" (1.2 × 2.5 cm) and cut stone is ½" × 1⅛" (1.4 × 2.8 cm)

tools

Wire cutters

Ruler

Pin vise

Tape

Fine-point marker

Square 3-stepped pliers

Flat-nose pliers

Double-barrel pliers

Medium chain-nose pliers

Fine chain-nose pliers

Round-nose pliers

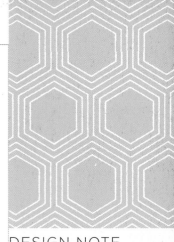

DESIGN NOTE

To assure consistency within a design that contains several similar components, make each component at the same time (repeating each step on each shape).

FORMULA: Circumference of stone + 2" (5 cm) = the length of wire. Width of stone + two wires = the number of frame wires needed.

1

Make a Drop Necklace Base (Figure 1). (See page 99.)

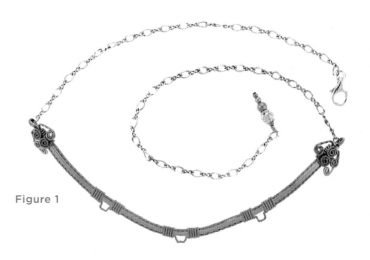

Figure 1

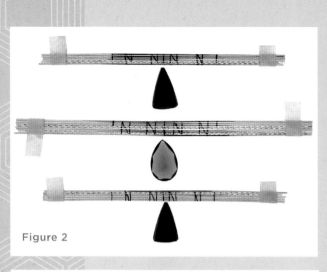

Figure 2

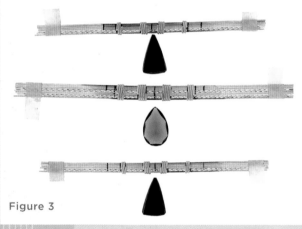

Figure 3

Figure 4

2

Straighten, clean, then measure and cut all necessary wires per stone. If desired, use a pin vise to individually twist a wire or two per frame. Bundle each set of frame wires together with one flush end and tape near each end. Measure and mark the center of the bundle and use the mark as a guide point. Refer to the Ornate Cabochon Bracelet Topping project on page 50 to determine where to make each set of wraps and mark accordingly (**Figure 2**).

3

Working from the center toward each end, use 6″ (15 cm) of 20- or 21-gauge half-round wire to wrap each marked segment (**Figure 3**).

4

Remove all tape and use appropriate shaping pliers/tools to form each frame bundle into the shape needed for its respective stone. (The drops pictured were shaped using square 3-stepped pliers, flat-nose pliers, and medium double-barrel pliers.) Fit each stone into its drop frame and tape the frame together, about ½″ (1.2 cm) up from the top of the stone (**Figure 4**).

TIP

When setting stones, a cushioned computer mouse pad makes a wonderful work surface that not only protects the stone from being scratched but because of the cushion feature, also works well to help set a stone while firmly pushing it into place.

5

Working either "on" or "off" the stones, use 2″ (5 cm) of the square half-hard wire to wrap each drop frame together. Begin with the hook headed toward the back of the drop and work from the junction of the frame up, two times to show. End with the wrap wire sticking straight out toward the front. Do not cut this wrap wire **(Figure 5)**.

6

Set each stone into its frame. Use flat-nose pliers on the back and chain-nose pliers on the front to make the pulls needed to secure each stone in its drop frame **(Figure 6)**. (See Ornate Cabochon Bracelet Topping, pages 51 and 52.)

7

Use the remaining wrap wire to complete one more wrap around the top, trimming it on the side, heading toward the back of the piece. Remove all tape and, except for the last two on the back, gently fan all wires on the top toward the front and sides. (If there are more wires than desired to use for decoration on the top, make them "disappear," as shown for the Ornate Cabochon Topping project, Step 12, page 52.) On each stone drop, trim the last two wires from the back of the frame to ⁵⁄₈″ (1.5 cm) **(Figure 7)**.

8

Working with the two wires just trimmed, measure ³⁄₈″ (1 cm) up from the top of the drop's wrap and mark. Working with each pair of wires as though they were one, place round-nose pliers on the ³⁄₈″ (1 cm) mark and roll these wires toward the front of the drop. Remove the pliers and trim the wire ends so they butt up against the top of the wrap **(Figure 8)**.

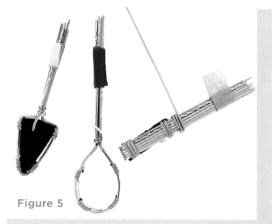

Figure 5

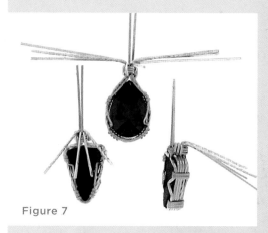

Figure 6

Figure 7

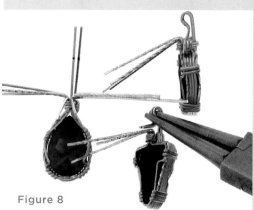

Figure 8

Figure 9

9

Slip the connection bail created in Step 8 over a connection loop on the necklace base. Use the next free wire toward the back to wrap the connection into place from one side across the front and around the back a minimum of two times to show. Trim and finish on the side of the wrap. Repeat connection procedure with each of the gem/cabochon drops, attaching one stone at a time and working from one side toward the other (Figure 9). Use the remaining free wires to decorate as desired, with beads, rosettes, etc. (Figure 10). See detail on pages 99 and 104.

NOTE: If a symmetrical design is desired, remember to mirror the wraps and decorations of the gem/cabochon drops from one side to the other.

Figure 10

tri-blue pendant

Vivian Huff used ideas from *Gem Drop Earrings* (page 68) to make this pretty pendant.

Finished size: $^5/_8$" x $1^7/_8$" (1.6 x 4.8 cm)

starry butte necklace

By combining techniques from the *Ornate Cabochon Topping* (page 49) and *Gem Drop Earrings* (page 68) Sonja Kiser created a unique agate necklace.

Finished size: $1^5/_8$" x $3^1/_4$" (4.1 x 8.3 cm)

neck COLLAR

This is a very basic design that can be utilized in a variety of ways. A single 12- or 14-gauge wire can easily be shaped into a collar with a hook on each end. The design below takes this idea one step further. Imagine using a base design such as the one below and adding segments such as those in the drop necklace pattern, beads, charms, or stone pendants. How about using three or even four or five wires and twisting them together? Amazing!

materials

F length of 14-gauge dead-soft wire

F length of 16-gauge round half-hard wire

tools

Flat-nose pliers

Medium chain-nose pliers

Double-barrel pliers

3-stepped pliers

Cutters

Ruler

Fine-point marker

Power wire twister

Finished Size: 17" (43 cm) circumference

DESIGN NOTE

Almost any combination of wire gauges and shapes will work for this project. Heavier wire will result in a sturdier finished product.

FORMULA: *Wire Length* (F) = desired neck length + 2" (5 cm) for base wire

NECK COLLAR

1

Clean, measure, and cut the base wire and a round wire the same length. Use a power drill to twist the square base wire, leaving 1 1/2" (3.7 cm) plain on each end in order to form hooks. Place the round wire next to the twisted square wire in the drill and twist the round wire around the square **(Figure 1)**.

2

Use flat-nose pliers to hold the ends of the two wires together and use chain-nose pliers to wrap the round wire around the square wire two times to show. Cut the round wire end off at a sharp angle, use a stone to file the end smooth, and tuck it around the twisted wire. Repeat on the opposite end of the collar, taking care to end on the same side as the first wrap **(Figure 2)**.

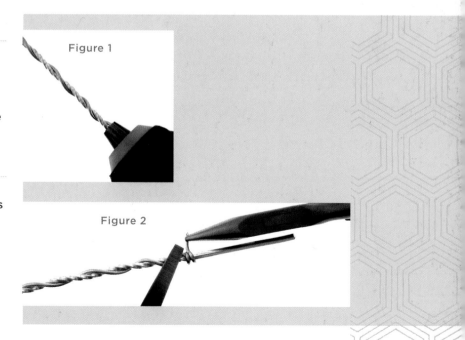

Figure 1

Figure 2

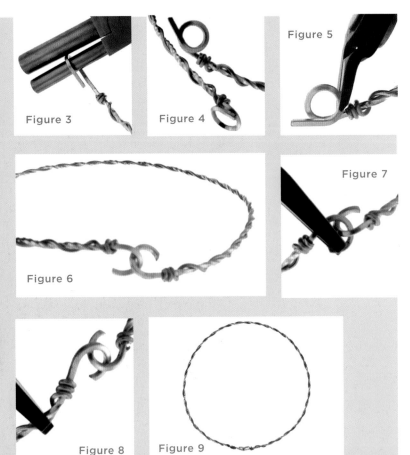

Figure 3

Figure 4

Figure 5

Figure 6

Figure 7

Figure 8

Figure 9

3

Use double-barrel pliers or a similar tool to shape a full circle at each end, parallel to the collar, one end up and one end down **(Figures 3 and 4)**. Trim each circle into the size hook desired with a sharp angle cut and file the ends **(Figure 5)**. Use a small metal coffee can or a neck mandrel to shape the collar, making sure to choose a round item that the collar wire will wrap around about one and one half times.

4

As the collar will more than likely be askew, use flat-nose pliers to adjust the hooks **(Figures 6 and 7)**. Use flat-nose pliers to put a slight bend into each end just before the hook, causing the collar to lay flat **(Figure 8)**. Finish forming the shape by hand while around your neck, adding a slight bend to fit over the collarbone **(Figure 9)**.

vintage swarovski

Suzanne Hollingsworth made this vintage style pendant by using techniques from *Gem Drop Earrings* (page 68).

circling fishes collar

Marie "Mint" Schlief unleashed her creativity by blending techniques from several projects to create this stunning collar: *Chevron Bracelet Base* (page 44), *Ornate Cabochon Topping* (page 49), and *Drop Necklace Base* (page 99).

Finished size: circumference (without chain) 16⅝" (42.2 cm); triangle of fish centerpiece 4½" x 3¼" (11.4 x 8.3 cm)

gold chain and lapis necklace

Cynthia Pilchard combined her modified version of a finished *Ornate Cabochon Bracelet* (pages 45 and 49) with techniques from the *Drop Necklace Base* (page 99) to make this lovely necklace.

Finished size of centerpiece: 6" x 2" (15 x 5 cm)

114

bonus project: FILIGREE FLOWER

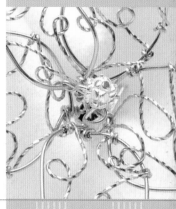

Sometimes I dream of what I could do if I would learn to solder. One of these fantasies is to make serious filigree designs. This flower is an example of what I call cold filigree. Make the flowers large or small, with many or few petals, and then shape the petals anyway you'd like. This project is meant to be a suggestion that can be reformulated to fit almost any size beads, pearls, and wire. The finished flower can be incorporated into many styles of head ornaments such as a comb, headband, or tiara. It can also become a hat pin, stickpin, ring, or used as an attachment on the Collar (page 110) or the Chevron Bracelet (page 48). Have fun with this design!

DESIGN NOTE

Use beads of metal, crystal, and/or pearl for a variety of flower looks. Find patterns and inspiration for your own flower designs by taking or finding pictures of flowers that you would like to imitate.

materials

21- or 22-gauge round, #8 spring-hard or half-hard wire for the frame wire for the petals (spring-hard wire is recommended so that the finished petals can be shaped and rearranged often, without fear of breakage).

24-gauge square half-hard wire for the filigree and the stamen

A variety of 2–4mm crystals or beads for the "dew drop" accents on the petals

One 3–6mm crystal or bead for the stamen

One 5, 6, or 8mm metal bead for the base

Finished Size: petals range in size from ⅝" × 1¾" (1.6 × 4.5 cm) to ⅞" × 2¼" (2.3 × 5.8 cm); the full flower is 3¾" × 4¼" (9.6 × 10.8 cm)

tools

Flat-nose pliers

Fine and medium chain-nose pliers

Fine and medium round-nose pliers

Wire cutters

Tape

Ruler

Forming pliers (such as double barrel)

Fine-point marker

Pin vise

Dremel with a diamond drill bit as it may be necessary to enlarge a metal bead hole to accommodate the number of petal wires desired

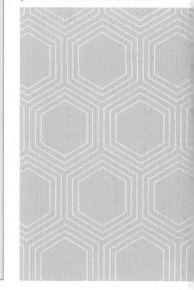

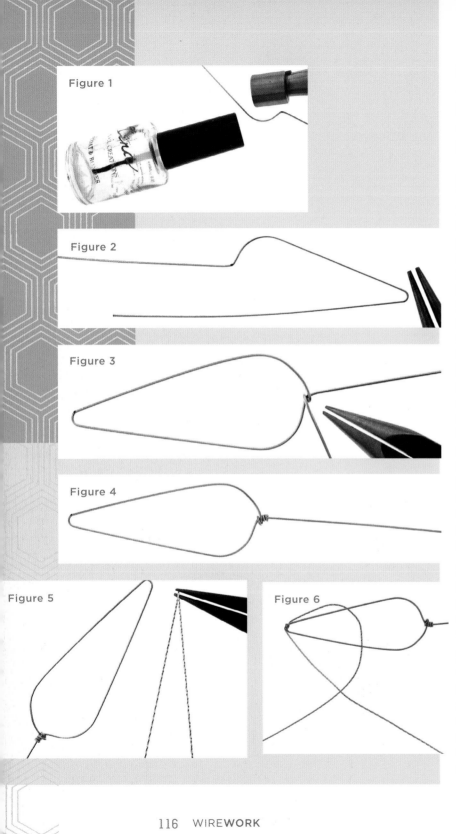

Figure 1

Figure 2

Figure 3

Figure 4

Figure 5

Figure 6

FORMULA: *Lily Petal* 3" (7.5 cm) (for the stem) + desired petal length × 2 + 1" (2.5 cm) = the length of each frame wire. (The project shown was made using five petals, each about $2\frac{1}{2}$" (6.2 cm) long.)

FILIGREE FLOWER

1

Form the petal frames. Straighten, clean, then measure and cut an 8" (20.2 cm) petal wire. Measure from one end of the wire the 3" (7.5 cm) needed for the stem and mark. Use flat-nose pliers to hold the wire just below the mark and use fingers to bend it at a 45° angle over the pliers' jaw. Measure $2\frac{1}{2}$" (6.2 cm) up from this bend and mark. Place larger round shaping pliers or a found item just above the 45° bend and curve the wire back toward itself **(Figure 1)**. Use smaller round-nose pliers to hold the petal wire at the second mark and use fingers to complete the bend back toward the stem **(Figure 2)**. Measure down $2\frac{1}{2}$" (6.2 cm) and mark. Use the same item as before to add a larger curve just before the new mark. At the last mark made, use chain-nose pliers to wrap the petal once around its other side and then around its stem two times to show **(Figure 3)**. Trim the wire.

2

Repeat Step 1 on as many petals as are planned for the finished flower, keeping in mind that all of the petals need not look alike **(Figure 4)**.

3

Weave the filigree. For a $2\frac{1}{2}$" (6.2 cm) long, narrow petal, start with a twisted 10" (25.2 cm) piece of 24-gauge square half-hard wire. Use round-nose pliers to bend this wire in half **(Figure 5)**. Place the curved center on the middle of the wire petal tip and wrap it around the petal two times **(Figure 6)**.

4

Continue weaving the twisted wire from one side of the petal to the other, using round-nose pliers to insert tiny loops to fill large spaces and threading on small beads where either color or dew drops are desired (**Figure 7**). Add more wire lengths if needed (**Figure 8**). Finish by wrapping the filigree wire ends around the bottom of the petal base and trim (**Figure 9**).

NOTE: As the twisted wire is teased and worked through the petal form, it will quite often take on a mind of its own, forming nice curves. My advice is to "go with the flow."

5

Create the stamen. Make one or more stamens for each flower. The wire should allow for a 3″ (7.5 cm) stem length, plus 1″ (2.5 cm) to account for the bead(s), plus another 1″ to 2″ (2.5 cm to 5 cm) for the height of the stamen, according to the flower being designed. Use one end of the wire to string the chosen bead, leaving about 1″ (2.5 cm) of wire above the bead. Use this wire end to wrap down around the bead and coil twice around the wire.

6

Assemble the flower. Use large-barrel pliers to slightly bend each petal toward its back (**Figures 10 and 11**). Insert all of the petal stems through a large—6mm or so—metal bead (**Figure 12**). Push the stamen wire(s) into the center of the petal wires through the base bead. Use one of the stamen wires to wrap all of the stem wires together immediately under the base bead (**Figure 13**).

7

Give the flower life! Use flat-nose pliers to tightly pull all petals down to fit snugly into the base bead. Arrange the petals and stamen as desired. Use a variety of rounded shaping tools to add the necessary curves to the bases and tips of the petals (**Figure 14**).

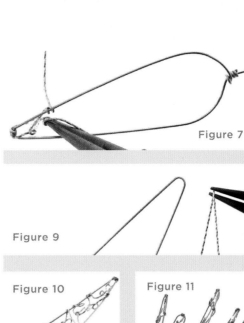
Figure 7

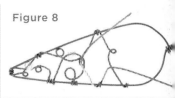
Figure 8

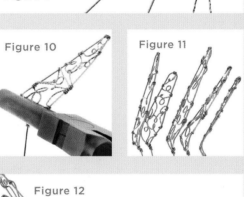
Figure 9

Figure 10

Figure 11

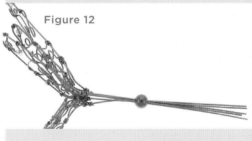
Figure 12

Figure 13

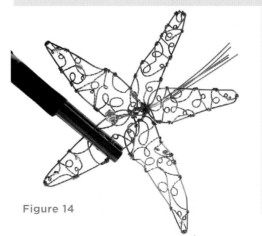
Figure 14

INSPIRATION GALLERY

I personally created all of the following articles of jewelry using a variety of the techniques shown throughout this book. It is my hope that these ideas will spark your creative juices and inspire you to experiment and play with more faceted stone and bead combinations. Just remember, designer pieces are nothing more than a wonderful collaboration of well-executed components. After all, inspiration comes from everywhere and every thing.

~Cougar

Hummingbird Scrimshaw Bracelet. Designed to show off this ivory scrimshaw by Mary W. Bailey, I made this bracelet using a combination of sterling silver and 14k gold-filled wire. The sterling pattern wire in the center was chosen to complement the garden theme.

Finished size of the decorative top: 2″ x 2¹/₈″ (5.1 x 5.4 cm)

Turquoise Chunk Bracelet. Interesting results can occur when large individual beads are used in the same manner as my Beads All Around Clasp Bangle, page 54. Try combining gold with turquoise (rather than silver) as a gentle way to "get out of the box."

Finished size (circumference): 7³/₄″ (19.7 cm)

Beaded Clasp Bangle (left). The Beads All Around Clasp Bangle pattern can be simplified to use just a single strand and one size of bead, shown here using 6mm round amethyst fashioned in argentium silver wire.

Finished size of the decorative top: 2³/₈″ x ⁵/₈″ (6 x 1.6 cm)

Golden Kite (below). Just about any shape or size faceted stone can be celebrated with the Orbit Prong Gemstone Pendant design, page 88, such as this lovely kite cut gold sapphire set in 14k gold-filled wire.

Finished size: ⁷/₈″ x 1³/₈″ (2.2 x 3.5 cm)

Victorian Bangle (above). Smaller cabochons like this 18x13mm gold sapphire can be featured in beautiful chevron bracelet designs. The rich look comes from combining argentium silver and 14k gold-filled wires.

Finished size of the decorative top: 3″ x ⁷/₈″ (7.6 x 2.2 cm)

Experiment with Rainbow Calsilica. This "experiment" was to combine different-size cabochons into a wearable piece of arm art. Adding a variety of complimentary beads brought the balance of the visual and the physical weight together.

Finished size of the decorative top center: 2⁷⁄₈" x 1¹⁄₂" (7.3 x 3.8 cm)

Marquis Bangle. Setting a marquis-cut stone can be a challenge when considering protection for the stones' points. The outer rims of the chevron bangle, fashioned in 14k gold-filled wire, protect this blue zircon.

Finished size of the decorative top: 2⁵⁄₈" x 1" (6.7 x 2.5 cm)

Firestar (right)

The Orbit Prong Gemstone Pendant pattern, page 88, can be artistically altered, as shown with this lab-grown ruby mounted in 14k gold-filled wire.

Finished size: 1⅛" x 1¾" (2.9 x 4.4 cm)

Sparkling Finger Bauble (above). It's a party on your finger! Crystals mixed in a variety of colors and sizes produce delightful results, using techniques from Filigree Pearl Ring, page 32.

Finished size: 1⅜" x 1" (3.5 x 2.5 cm)

Yum Drops (right). Faceted tourmaline in 14k gold-filled wire. Gem Drop Earrings, page 68, can be made using stones in a multitude of cuts, such as these pear-cut, faceted tourmalines in 14k gold-filled wire.

Finished size: ⅜" x 1⅝" (1 x 4.1 cm)

Variations on the Filigree Pearl Ring. More casual or dressy styles will emerge when different gemstone beads are substituted for the pearl.

Finished size of the pearl and amber rings: 1³/₈" x ³/₄" (3.5 x 1.9 cm). Finished size of the kyanite ring: 1¹/₂" x ⁵/₈" (3.8 x 1.6 cm).

Amethyst Drops. Simplifying the Gem Drop Earrings pattern, page 68, will produce the versatile yet elegant design shown here using amethyst in sterling silver.

Finished size: ¹/₂" x 2¹/₈" (1.3 x 5.4 cm)

Small Filigree Flower with Pearls. Filigree Flowers, page 114, can be made in any shape or size desired. Accented with pearls, this is my dahlia rendition.

Finished size: 2¹/₄" (5.7 cm)

Blue Fantasy. Special stones deserve special settings, as shown by using the Orbit Prong Gemstone Pendant pattern, page 88, to mount this 36ct fantasy-cut blue topaz in 14k solid gold.

Finished size: 1¹/₄" x 1⁵/₈" (3.2 x 4.1 cm)

Fire and Ice Necklace.
Utilizing the curvature gained from
hammering heavy 14k gold-filled wire,
adding a lab-grown ruby, and accent-
ing with freshwater pearls, shows that
elegance can be achieved when using a
wide range of materials and techniques.

**Finished size of the pendant: 3" x 4"
(7.6 x 10.2 cm)**

Fire and Ice Earrings. The matching
earrings can be enjoyed alone. Combining loose connections with the
hammered texture give them a lot of
motion and sparkle.

Finished size: $^7/_8$" x $3^1/_2$" (2.2 x
8.9 cm)

Egyptian Summer. The Drop Necklace Base Design pattern, page 99, can be restyled by adding or subtracting width wires and by using stones cut in different shapes. This is my original prototype, fashioned using violet and gold lab-grown sapphires in 14k gold-filled wire.

Finished size: $5^{3}/_{4}$" x $1^{3}/_{4}$" (14.6 x 4.4 cm)

SUPPLIES

Brandywine Jewelry Supply
brandywinejewelrysupply.com
Wire, snap-set findings, beads, gemstones,
cabochons, findings, packaging, etc.

Kingsley North Inc.
kingsleynorth.com
Lapidary supplies, cabochons, Speed Brite Jewelry
Cleaners, tools, and equipment.

Rio Grande
(800) 545-6566
7500 Bluewater Rd. NW
Albuquerque, NM 87121
riogrande.com
Tools and equipment, display and packaging, and
gemstones and findings.

Sierra Madres Mining Co.
John Bajoras
138 Main St.
Gloucester, MA 01930
(978) 283-8811
Neyla@villagesilversmith.net
Custom and designer cabochons, slabs, rough, and
minerals.

SII Findings
siifindings.com
Copper, Bali silver, Thai silver, sterling silver, gold-
filled, 14k gold, and vermeil findings and beads and a
large variety of chain by the foot.

TB Hagstoz
709 Samson St.
Philadelphia, PA 19106
(800) 922-1006
(215) 922-7126 fax
hagstoz.com
Argentium, sterling, copper, gold-filled, and 14k and
18k gold wire, refining, and tools.

Business Related

beadingdaily.com
Free projects, forums, and links to related magazines,
books, and suppliers.

craftsreport.com
Written by and for artists of all mediums, informative
website includes discussion board, show information,
and more.

home-jewelry-business-success-tips.com/jewelry-
making-forums.html
Links to many different jewelry-making and jewelry-
business forums

Magazines

Colored Stone
colored-stone.com
Your guide to selling, style, and sources in the colored
gemstone industry.

The Crafts Report
craftsreport.com
Established in 1975, this is a monthly business magazine for the crafts professional.

Rock & Gem
rockngem.com
Once you start reading about all the exciting things
rockhounds are doing these days, you can't help but
join in.

Step by Step Wire Jewelry
stepbystepwire.com
Packed with detailed and illustrated how-to projects,
this magazine is for wire jewelry makers of all levels.

INDEX

Arken-stone 17
Arnao, Dottie 97

angle flush cutters 15

Bailey, Mary W. 97, 118
bails 81
beads, adding 55–61
bracelet wire shaping 40–43

cabochon, setting 50–53
chain-nose pliers 14
clasp, hook-and-eye 42
cleaning, jewelry 17

dead-soft wire 13
double-barrel pliers 16
drill, power 16
drops, making 99–103

earring design 63
ends, smoothing wire 20

filigree 36–37, 115–117
flat-nose pliers 15
forming tools 16–17

Gentry, Jill 37

half-hard wire 12–13
half-round wire 13
Hollingsworth, Suzanne 112
hook-and-eye clasp 42
Huff, Vivian 109

jewelry cleaning machine 17

kerf 14, 15
Kiser, Sonja 109

Lingerfelt, Sherrie 87
Luttrell, K. 53

mandrel, ring 17
marker, pen 17

pendant, making 89–96
pliers 14–15, 16
Pilchard, Cynthia 113

ring sizing 21
round-nose pliers 15

Schneck, Lindi Lou 87
Schlief, Marie "Mint" 113
shank, ring 20
shaping, bracelet 40–43
sizing, ring 21
smooth-jaw pliers see chain-nose pliers
snap-set heads 75
square wire 13
stones, setting in snap-set heads 75–76

tape 17
3-stepped pliers 16, 17

vise, pin 16

wire 12–13, 81
wire ends, smoothing 20
wire gauge chart 12
Wurm, Sandra W. 53

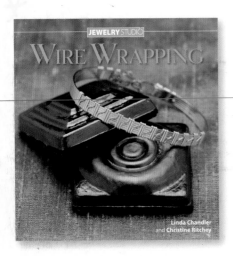
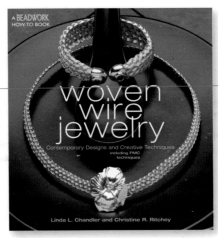